humphrey lyttelton it just occurred to me...

the reminiscences & thoughts of Chairman Humph

Praise for *It Just Occurred to Me...*

'Reading the Chairman's passing memories enriched a free weekend in the English countryside for me, as would reading Proust, Dickens or Melville. A damn sight funnier. Humph is cool, Humph is *now!*'
– Pete Townshend

'One of the most charming and laugh-out-loud funny books I have ever had the pleasure to read.'
– Sholto Byrnes, *Independent on Sunday*

'I found so much to laugh at and admire that I read it twice in the space of a fortnight.'
– Charles Spencer, the *Spectator*

'Undertake a nationwide poll to find Britain's best-loved entertainer and surely Humphrey Lyttelton would come close to topping it.'
– *Saga*

'Lyttelton's humorous memoir is hugely entertaining.'
– The *Good Book Guide*

HUMPHREY LYTTELTON is descended from a long line of land-owning, political, military, clerical, scholastic and literary forebears. Not a musician among them. He was born on 23 May 1921, in Eton College, where his father was a famous housemaster, and where he was subsequently educated. During the Second World War he served as an officer in the Grenadier Guards and on demobilization studied for two years at Camberwell Arts School. Humph formed his first jazz band in 1948, which became the leading traditional jazz band in Britain, with a high reputation in Europe. His composition 'Bad Penny Blues', recorded for Parlophone in 1956, was the first British jazz record to get into the Top Twenty. He and his band remain as in-demand as ever. Every Monday night since 1967 Humph has written and presented BBC Radio 2's The Best of Jazz. Nowadays, when people say 'I enjoy your radio show ...', they are as likely to mean the anarchic award-winning BBC Radio 4 panel game I'm Sorry I Haven't A Clue. Humph has written eight books and composed two hundred tunes. In what few leisure moments he has, he enjoys bird-watching and is a keen amateur calligrapher. In 1990 he was appointed President of the Society For Italic Handwriting. He has been awarded Honorary Doctorates in Music, Letters and the Arts at the universities of Warwick (1987), Loughborough (1988), Durham (1989), Keele (1992), Hertford (1995) and de Montfort (1997).

humphrey lyttelton it just occurred to me...

the reminiscences
& thoughts of
Chairman
Humph

ROBSON
BOOKS

First published the United Kingdom in hardback in 2006

This paperback edition published in 2007 by
Robson Books
10 Southcombe Street
London
W14 0RA

An imprint of Anova Books Company Ltd

ISBN 10: 1 90579 817 2
ISBN 13: 9781905798179

A CIP catalogue record for this book is available from the British
Library.

10 9 8 7 6 5 4 3 2 1

Reproduction by Anorax Imaging Ltd, Leeds
Typeset by SX Composing DTP, Rayleigh, Essex
Printed and bound by Creative Print & Design, Ebbw Vale, Wales

This book can be ordered direct from the publisher.
Contact the marketing department, but try your bookshop first.

www.anovabooks.com

In memory of Jill

INTRODUCTION

As someone who is often called upon to present concerts or similar events, I have many times uttered the words 'our guest tonight needs no introduction . . .'

So far as this book is concerned, it's not just that it doesn't need one. It's almost impossible to write one. How did I come to write it? Why that title? You might as well ask, when I've just played five choruses of the St Louis Blues on the trumpet, 'What have you just played, and why?' It's not for nothing that I have, for nigh on thirty years, been chairman of a BBC radio show called *I'm Sorry I Haven't A Clue*. (Actually it very nearly is for nothing, but that's between me and the Corporation).

It just occurred to me that writing this book has been very similar to blowing an extended solo on the trumpet following thoughts wherever they've led, through a jungle of ideas and memories, quotations and clichés, high notes, blue notes and, no doubt, a few wrong notes, for which I apologise in advance. On second thoughts, no, I don't. You'll get precious few right notes if you worry about hitting wrong notes.

There will be quite frequent interruptions by someone who calls himself Chairman Humph. Why do I allow this? Because it's nice to know that there is someone else, if only an alter ego, to blame if things go wrong.

Humphrey Lyttelton

P.S. If you're from the BBC, I was only joking. Well, you have to, don't you?

IT JUST OCCURRED TO ME . . .

> Does the average man get enough sleep? What is 'the average man'? What is 'enough sleep'? What is 'does'?
>
> Robert Benchley, opening one of his humorous articles in the
> *New Yorker*

And what an opening! It's one of many things in print and in conversation that I wish I had thought of myself. But, as the neglectful picnicker so rightly says when berated for leaving the tin-opener out of the hamper, you can't think of everything.

It is, nevertheless, just the sort of opening I need to get this book off the launching pad. When I say to people that I'm working on a book, the first question that comes back at me like a Federer return of service is 'Oh, really – what's it about?' If I tell the truth and say that it's a random hotchpotch of thoughts and experiences that have occurred to me over the years, they tend to utter that meaningful syllable 'Mmmm . . .' and turn away with a thought-bubble appearing above their heads saying: 'I'm not sure I want to read a hotchpotch – give me a book that's got a beginning, a middle and an end.' It's hardly more enticing if I adopt a cunning expression and say, 'Ah, you'll have to read it and see,' suggesting as it does that they must plough through two hundred or so pages in the hope that the answer will be revealed at the very end, like the denouement in a whodunnit.

Nevertheless, a hotchpotch of thought and memories it is. If that sounds vague, then I must ask, what else but vague are random thoughts and memories? There's no butler of the mind to usher them in – 'A thought to see you, sir – it wishes to discuss

1

existentialism.' No, mostly they just wander in and out of the room uninvited, like children, cats or hospital cleaners. For instance, it just occurred to me as I read these paragraphs through, that in the last few minutes I've written the word 'nevertheless' twice without having the slightest idea what it means. So I've taken the dictionary off the shelf and it says, 'for all that, notwithstanding'. I'm sorry, but I haven't the faintest idea what they mean either, now I come to look at it. How easy it is for thoughts to run away with you, and you do have to be careful. One doesn't want to incur the charge of 'piling Pelion on Ossa'. I first heard that quotation when I was working on the *Daily Mail* as a cartoonist in the late forties.

The job came about through what I suppose could be termed the Young Pals' Act. In the band known as George Webb's Dixielanders, wherein I made my debut as an ensemble member (or, as we say in the trade, 'sideman'), the clarinettist was Wally Fawkes, who doubled as an illustrator on the *Daily Mail* under the pen-name of Trog. When I formed my own band in 1948, Wally came in as a founder member. To compound the association, during those years we were both students at the Camberwell School of Arts and Crafts. At one point in these events, Wally tipped me off that he was about to start a daily strip-cartoon on the *Mail* (it became the long-running 'Flook' saga) and that his job livening up the columns with little pen-and-ink drawings would fall vacant. His words were on the lines of, 'Get some samples of your stuff together and go in to see the Features editor. I've already primed him.' He had indeed. The man barely glanced at my work before saying, 'You start tomorrow.' And that led to eight years on the *Daily Mail* during which I graduated to pocket cartoonist and, for a year or two, librettist for 'Flook'.

It was during my stint on the *Mail* that I absorbed one of the prime rules of journalism, which I will promote here to a position among the thoughts of Chairman Humph that pepper this book:

Whatever assignment you are offered, say 'yes' first and
learn about it afterwards.

Chairman Humph in advisory mode

There was a one-off concert held in London that brought together
the Ted Heath Orchestra and the classical French horn virtuoso,
Denis Brain. Knowing of my jazz association, the deputy editor of
the paper sent me off to review it for the Features page. I have
little recollection of the music or what I said about it. But it led to
my being offered a regular column in the paper writing reviews of
gramophone records of all kinds.

Years later, following the above precept, I found myself writing
restaurant reviews in *Harpers & Queen* magazine. In a moment of
self-doubt, I said to George Melly, who had been doing the film
reviews for the *Observer*, 'I'm sure they're going to find out one
day that I know nothing about it.' His answer was convoluted but
true: 'Yes, but in my experience, by the time they find out you
know nothing about it, you will know something about it.'

My method of acquiring belated knowledge about the
classical music which I was given to review in the *Mail* was to
plunder any articles I could find in specialist magazines –
predominantly the *Gramophone* – and rewrite them in my own
authoritative words. Although I was in my mid-twenties when I
came out of the wartime army, I was in the first flush of youth
so far as writing was concerned and, with the arrogance of
youth, I picked on all the contentious bits and exaggerated
them, lambasting conductors and recording companies alike.
After two or three columns, I was sent for by the deputy editor
and rebuked for, as he said, 'piling Pelion on Ossa'. I had never
come across that phrase before but I got the gist and was duly
humbled. When, years later, I looked it up in the *Oxford
Dictionary of Quotations*, I found out that the man had got the
quotation upside down.

Three times they endeavoured to pile Ossa on Pelion, no
less, and to roll leafy Olympus on top of Ossa: three times
our Father scattered the heaped-up mountains with a
thunderbolt.

Virgil, writing about mountains in his fanciful way

Had I known that my little column had, albeit unwittingly, been
compared to the cataclysmic events that Virgil was describing, I
would have been quite flattered. As it was, the deputy editor's
rebuke rumbled on, changing the subject and teaching me, in the
process, another ground-rule of popular journalism.

He reminded me that my column took up about eight column-
inches on the Features page of the paper, an area designed as an
oasis of light, entertaining relief for our readers amidst the
weightier matters discussed on the news and comment pages.
'The last thing those readers want,' he said, 'is someone taking up
precious space fulminating over some conductor who has taken
the Scherzo movement of Beethoven's Seventh too fast. All that is
for the specialist magazines.' (Little did he know that that was
where it came from.) 'You'd do better to aim your piece at
someone who hates classical music and doesn't own a gramophone. If you can get HIM to read your column, you're doing
something useful.'

It was advice that I readily embraced when that letter came
from *Queen* magazine asking if I would write a one-off 'guest'
restaurant review. Their regular writer, the outspoken Linda
Blandford, had spoken out once too often about some lofty
establishment whose owners were threatening to sue, so she had
been hastily transferred to a safer department of the magazine. In
accordance with the advice about journalistic assignments stated
earlier by Chairman Humph, I said 'yes' to the offer and set about
cobbling together a piece that used up the handful of restaurants
I knew well from family outings.

It led, rather alarmingly, to eight years as restaurant reviewer for what became *Harpers & Queen*. At the end of it I left, feeling rather sick. I had picked up a couple of Food-writer of the Year Awards along the way, so I must have done something right. But if anything, that reinforced the uneasy feeling that I was, in fact, a fraud. But food-writing (the very terminology looks more and more absurd the longer you stare at it) was altogether less ponderous then than it is today. The journalist, novelist and historian Raymond Postgate had founded the Good Food Club in the mid-fifties to be a focal point for lovers of food and drink across the nation. Their amateur reports were invited and published in the *Good Food Guide*, the pages of which exuded a kind of fraternal enthusiasm. It was not called the *Good Food Guide* for nothing. It was Postgate's idea that it would indeed be a guide to let readers know where, in whatever benighted city or town they found themselves, they could find the best food. Here's a thought in passing:

> Nowadays, it's still possible to find oneself in an Indian restaurant the very interior of which arouses deep foreboding. To establish peace of mind, be sure to order up poppadams first before committing yourself to other dishes. If, when they arrive, the first nibble suggests they have been deep-fried in rancid badger-fat, make your excuses and leave. Cooked in the same pan, the rest of the meal will shuttle you into intensive care quicker than you can say 'murghee mossala'.
>
> Chairman Humph, the former food-writer in cautionary mode

Though my *Harper's* articles were largely concerned with restaurants in London or the Home Counties, I wrote them in much the same helpful spirit as the early *Good Food Guide*, always bearing in mind the reader in Carlisle, in the dentist's waiting room or under the hairdryer, who travels south perhaps once in a decade and is on a permanent diet. In the process, I found myself enjoying the writing more and more, the food less and less. George Melly told me that he and his band used to buy the magazine to read my pieces on their band bus, taking bets as to how many columns I would cover each week before actually getting round to mentioning a restaurant.

And that leads me to another reason why I began to recoil from the whole *bon viveur* nonsense in which I was becoming embroiled:

'Fifty Thousand Flies Can't Be Wrong.'

The late Ronnie Scott's generic term for the roadside transport cafes in which touring musicians took their sustenance before motorways arrived

The fact is that any touring musician, then and now, who adopts a high-minded attitude to gastronomy will starve to death. My experiences travelling around with a band at all hours of the day and night instilled in me, early on, a principle which, as a food-writer, I had to suppress in my *Harpers & Queen* days.

The term 'good food' is not an absolute, it depends on circumstances.

Chairman Humph in argumentative mode

An interviewer once asked me, licking his lips in expectation, where I would choose to go and what I would eat, to unwind after a concert or a long day in front of a microphone. When I answered, 'Home, to a bowl of cornflakes and a Kit Kat', his expression ping-ponged rapidly between shock-horror and the realisation that he might have stumbled on a minor scoop. I could have gone further, recalling that while driving home down the M1 in its early days, I had often drooled in anticipation of the splendid egg, sausage, beans and chips dispensed through the night at the Granada Service Area, Toddington. The team of West

Indian ladies there knew just when to rescue the eggs from the sizzling hell of the griddle.

In later years, I have avoided night driving, staying over in roadside hotels – most of which have been crushed by the onward march of takeovers and mergers into a dire uniformity.

There's no doubt about it – food is one of the pillars of *joie de vivre*. It's true – why talk about it?

Albert Rizk, Lebanese restaurateur who entertained my band to bursting point at lunch in his little Tivoli Restaurant outside Beirut. At a rough estimate, he himself tipped the scales in the region of twenty stone

There is, it must be said, very little *joie de vivre* to be gleaned nowadays from the fare available in hotels when the weary musician returns from work at dead of night. Room-service menus, if they exist, will usually offer dishes that can be ordered after 11 p.m. But most of them seem to have been specially selected to sabotage the subsequent night's sleep, consisting of a choice between curry or a 'pasta bake' that arrives steaming under a duvet of molten cheese. I can only think that this lethal choice was devised by a deranged insomniac, offering as it does a night of life-threatening reflux in the first instance and ghastly nightmares in the second. But I didn't come here to become a food-writer all over again, especially as we seem to have reached, by *reductio ad absurdum*, the topic of sandwiches.

Once, in recent times, finding myself in a hotel that offered no room service of any kind, I rang Reception. A girl, young in voice, answered and I asked if sandwiches were available. They were, and the following dialogue ensued:

'What sandwiches do you have?'
'Ham, roast beef or cheena.'
'What was that last one?'
'Cheena.'

'I don't know what that is.'

'You know, CHEENA.'

At this point I began to feel my age. She was clearly offering some fashionable product that the whole world knew about except me. I became testy.

'But I don't know what cheena is!'

She wasn't sounding too relaxed herself.

'It's a fish!'

'WHAT SORT OF FISH?'

'CHEENA!!!'

It was very late at night, and I was not at my brightest. But the sinking pebble did eventually hit the river bed and, since tuna is more digestible than the other options, I did indeed order a round. The episode does raise a serious point about contemporary speech. I have a family friend of long standing, Caroline Cole, who in mid-life is studying for a degree in Medieval English at Oxford, a discipline which spills over into the English language in general. It's a subject about which we often argue over a friendly meal. We belong to opposing camps, with myself upholding principles about grammar and pronunciation learned at my father's knee (George Lyttelton having been a schoolmaster who, in his time, numbered among the pupils in his literature classes George Orwell, Aldous and Julian Huxley, Christopher Hollis and other literary lions who passed through Eton College).

Caroline belongs to the school which insists that English, as a living language, is constantly developing and should not be inhibited by pedantic rules. We once clashed over the contemporary habit, which has spread across barriers of class and generation and even nationality, of dropping the letter 't' in favour of a weak glottal stop that converts the word 'Saturday' into 'Sa'urday'. (With a name like Lyttelton, I have had to respond to its translation into Lew'on – to rhyme with Isaac New'on – or face excommunication from a large section of the English-speaking world). In our argument, I cited the word 'charity', and she put up a stout defence of 'chari'y'. With malice aforethought I asked her to apply the 'new' pronunciation to the word 'chastity'. For the rest of the evening she kept returning to 'chas'i'y' but eventually got the giggles and had to concede the point. I held in reserve a story that might have clinched it earlier. Another friend, a retired deputy head teacher, told me that a colleague of hers, crossing the school playground, came on some small boys who had split into teams and were shying stones at a tin can. As she passed, one of the boys pointed excitedly at a successful teammate and claimed loudly, "e'i'i'!"

If one makes the not far-fetched assumption that the primary purpose of language is to communicate, then it's surely not pedantry to suggest that words should be pronounced in a way that is comprehensible. If I am careering along a motorway hoping that my car radio will warn me of any impending disruption, it's not helpful to be told by a traffic reporter that there are 'keys on the raid ahead'. In the split second that it takes to translate that into 'queues on the road ahead' I could be straight up the back end of a lorry.

Some people lay at the door of Australian soap operas the blame for the widespread demotion of the noble syllable 'oo' into something squeezed out of the front of the mouth, turning 'news' into 'knees' and 'views' into 'vees'. But the ailment once described by a wit as 'Irritating Vowel Syndrome' is not confined to any social class. As a corrective to any unseemly rush of pedantry to the head, there is plenty of archive material in the form of old films and newsreels to remind us that it was once 'standard' among judges, Pathé News commentators, film actors and other educated people to pronounce, for instance, the word 'adversary' as 'edversary'. Flashbacks to the Nuremburg trial in 1945–6 reveal the then Sir Geoffrey Lawrence QC (later Lord Oaksey), the senior presiding judge at the Nuremburg Trial, sentencing the Nazi war criminals, not once but repeatedly, to 'death by henging'.

That was, and rarely still is, just one of several upper-class aberrations. The quacking, silly-ass accent assumed by actors and

comedians to portray 'toffs' is in real life a rarity. Among a variety
of public school accents, there is one that restores the balance in
favour of the 'oo' sound by using it to the almost total exclusion
of all others, turning words such 'Wimbledon' and 'Bristol' into
'Woombledon' and 'Broostle'. I remember Prime Minister
Anthony Eden, at the time of the Suez crisis, telling an anxious
nation in an orgy of vowel mangling, 'We will do oovrythoong
we cairn to protect our vah-ital oonterests.' I must leave to others
to judge whether I speak with a recognisable Old Etonian accent.
I deny it, but I would, wouldn't I? Without consciously trying, I
seem to have shed, at some stage along the way, the usage of 'orf'
(in place of 'off') with which I was brought up. Indeed, I once,
in my argumentative youth, scored a rare, if not unique, victory
over my father in the matter of language.

It was in the early fifties, a stroppy period in my life. I was then at
art school, bearded and dressed in the style that in more recent times
has been designated as Grunge. My father was clearly destabilised
when I first appeared thus at what had become the family home in
Suffolk. One morning at the breakfast table, when I had aired some
no doubt half-baked left-wing ideas, he said, 'I hope you're not
turning into one of those French Socialists – all beard and belly.' (He
himself was conservative with a small 'c'. I once asked him why he
took the *New Statesman* on a regular subscription. His answer was,
'Because it's good to keep hatred alive.')

One of his pupils and a contemporary of mine at school, Simon
Phipps, had become an eminent cleric frequently seen on
television. When, in another encounter over the porridge, I
declared myself irritated by his frequent references to 'the Crorss',
my father leapt to his defence, claiming that the staccato 'Cross'
was no better. With a thrust as effective as my subsequent
wielding of the word 'chastity', I challenged him with the line
from a poem by one Caroline Norton in the seventeenth century,
which so often does service as an epitaph. Understandably
unwilling to mouth the words 'Not Lorst But Gorn Before', my

father got up from the table and left the room, clearing his throat loudly as if to renounce the whole conversation.

I must temper the foregoing by emphasising here the enormous benefit I derived from being the son of a schoolmaster who specialised in English. It was at his knee that I learned many of the principles of language, spelling and pronunciation that have since been blown away by the winds of populism, bringing confusion where there should be clarity.

I remember him demonstrating the tricky question as to what should follow the word 'different' by putting two pencils on the table parallel to each other, saying 'different FROM' as he moved them apart, 'similar TO' as he moved them closer together. It was a useful visual *aide mémoire*.

> Nowadays, encouraged by lexicographers who have surrendered to the theory that they have a duty to follow popular usage rather than inform it, 'different to' has almost universally triumphed over logic. Happily, we pedants are still free to differ to it. I beg your pardon, from it.
>
> Chairman Humph in didactic mode

To my great delight, I found, not very long ago, a paragraph in a so-called quality newspaper that exemplifies perfectly the corrosive effect of mispronunciation. It was written at the time of a notorious sleaze scandal. I quote now from the cutting, which I took eagerly and pasted in a notebook:

> The new disclosure puts the suitability of Mr Hamilton's candidature back on top of the political agenda only days after ministers were beginning to succeed in diffusing the issue after the Tatton Tories had readopted him.

Had the reporter observed the difference in pronunciation between 'diffuse' and 'defuse', he would not have written a sentence that conveyed a meaning diametrically opposed to that which he intended. There was a time when the latter word would have been spelt 'de-fuse', and I question whether the frequent banishment of the hyphen by editors and literary pundits, presumably in the interests of simplification, is altogether wise. It would serve today as a bastion against the invasive and intensely irritating pronunciation of the word 'research' as 're-search', and subsequently 're-course', 're-source', 're-spite', 're-lapse' and other now familiar aberrations that set alarm bells clanging in the brain of a pedant.

The disease has become epidemic. I have an old 1969 edition of the *Pocket Oxford Dictionary* which makes a clear distinction between the prefix 're' with a short accent, and the longer 'ree', the latter generally meaning 'again'. Current dictionaries give both as an option, which defies common sense for two reasons. One is that separating 'to research' from 'to ree-search' unequivocally makes it easier for someone learning the language, whether child or adult, to deduce the meaning of an unfamiliar word from the way its component parts are spoken. The other is that to juggle arbitrarily with pronunciation can play havoc with poetry. The six opening lines from Philip Larkin's poem, 'Last Will And Testament', contain a stark warning of what will happen if the 'ree' virus spreads further.

> Anxious to publicise and pay our dues
> Contracted here, we, Bernard Noel Hughes
> And Philip Arthur Larkin, do desire
>
> To requite and to reward those whom we choose;
> To thank our friends, before our time expire,
> And those whom, if not friends, we yet admire.

Now try 'ree-quite' and 'ree-ward'.
QED: *Quod erat demonstrandum* – a useful way to clinch the argument. At Eton, I learnt Latin and Greek. Though it took no

more than an eventful decade for the details to slip through the floorboards of my mind, I have never regarded those years of construing great chunks of them (construe – there's a quaint old word) as a waste of time. Some French sage once said, when asked if it was necessary to know Latin and Greek, 'No, but it's necessary to have forgotten them.' *Pourquoi?* Let's turn to a higher authority.

> The survival of the 'dead' languages, Latin and Greek, in the framework of contemporary English offers the only positive proof of life after death.
>
> Chairman Humph, in provocative mode

It follows that in dredging back through memories of old schooldays to recognise the Latin or Greek components of current words, you can avoid making a prat of yourself on *The Weakest Link*.

I seem to be getting heated, so while I go and run my head under a cold tap, here are two pedant-disarming aberrations of speech that I cherish.

In concert hall foyers or jazz festival compounds, people sometimes dash up to make hasty comments as the band leaves. They have no time to collect their thoughts and, as they hurry away, their step often falters as they realise they have just uttered complete gibberish. In the circumstances I warm to them for it.

A lady rushed up as I crossed a theatre foyer to leave after a band concert. She stood in front of me and said breathlessly, 'Mr Lyttelton, if you look as good as you play, you're doing jolly well!'

Again, a shy young man approached me at an open-air festival to get a CD signed. As I scribbled, he gushed, 'I listen to all your radio shows – this is the first time I've seen you in the flesh and your voice is much more recognisable now that I've heard it.'

*

I spent, now I come to think of it, most of my formative years in the doghouse. The memory is reinforced by a photograph which has survived of myself in my mid-teens wearing the Eton school uniform. Top hat, tailcoat, waistcoat and a rather ridiculous neck-piece (a horizontal strip of folded starched paper that doesn't merit the description of a tie) did little to flatter a youth growing un-symmetrically to an eventual six-foot-three. We had to look after our top hats, using a sort of velvet pad to maintain the sheen which, if neglected, tended to become coarse and unruly, like the coat of an ailing cat. It doesn't take a forensic expert to detect, in the photograph, that my top hat has a large dent on the left-hand side.

Footnote (literally): Around my eightieth birthday, I had a problem with my feet. The orthopaedist (I refuse to use the new term podiatrist. It suggests that one's feet are wrong in the head, a concept that only Picasso could have entertained) used a sophis-ticated camera that, as I strode across a sheet of plate glass embedded in the consulting-room floor, took 250 snaps of myself in motion. Subsequently a report came back from the analyst to say, 'Mr Lyttelton is seriously asymmetrical.' I bow to the judgement.

The Eton College curriculum involved regular end-of-term examinations known as Trials, the results of which were received by parents through the post just as an offspring was beginning to enjoy the escapism that holidays afforded. I can still re-enact in my mind one breakfast-time scene. My father had just opened the letter from my housemaster, Cyril Butterwick, which contained the information that I had scored two marks out of a possible hundred for my Maths paper. I and my older sister Diana had by then graduated from the upper regions of the house to breakfast with the grown-ups, leaving the three younger sisters in the care of Nanny and nursery-maids upstairs. I had, on this occasion, arrived late at the table, and saw with some dread that the envelope bearing Cyril Butterwick's neat scrawl had been opened. When I came into the room, my mother and sister, acting I assume upon premonition, got up and left.

As soon as I sat down, my father, who had up till then been hidden behind *The Times* (a broadsheet then, of course) brought the paper down and crumpled it explosively in his massive hands as if it were tissue-paper. It was a theatrical gesture that so startled me that the subsequent tongue-lashing seemed almost an anti-climax. I remain unsure to this day whether the rage was wholly genuine or stoked-up to suit the occasion. My later experience as a father, often called on to react suitably to an offence committed while I was away on tour (the 'Just Wait Till Your Father Gets Back' syndrome) admits that as a possibility. But it fulfilled its purpose and added to my belief at that time that I was a scruffy and bone-idle waste of space.

If my memory of Latin and Greek rapidly became vestigial when I left school, a vast swathe of my learning of mathematics was totally expunged. I must have known once what a logarithm is, since hours were devoted to installing it in my head. The what, why and wherefore, however, have vanished, leaving a void. Everything about algebra has long gone. I can derive more coherent meaning from a stanza of wordless scat-singing by Louis Armstrong or Ella Fitzgerald than a line of algebraic equation. Of geometry, some useful stuff about angles and shapes hangs about, though I've had to reach for the dictionary to spell 'hypotenuse'. I'm glad that I have retained some rudimentary knowledge of trigonometry. It's nice to know that when the night winds are howling outside, my neighbour's pine tree is not going to crash though the ceiling of my bedroom while I sleep.

Enter, unbidden and perhaps surprisingly, another thought, this one expressed by Lord Acton in a letter in 1887:

> Power tends to corrupt and absolute power corrupts absolutely.
>
> Lord Acton, writing to Bishop Mandell Crichton

The words 'tends to' are usually omitted when this quotation is called into use. I am happy to restore them since they allow for exceptions – my wise, tolerant and scrupulous father among them. Stretching the word 'corrupt' to embrace going completely barmy, it has not been difficult to find confirmation of his lordship's judgment in the world around us. Starting at the apex of barminess, the posturing of Hitler on his podium and Mussolini on his balcony gave clear evidence that 'absolute' power had sent them 'absolutely' off their respective trolleys.

Lodged in my mind is a small incident in a gents' lavatory in Italy during World War II. It must have been during a lull in the Salerno landing of 1943 in which I was involved. I found myself in the lavatory standing, as one does, next to an Italian civilian similarly engaged. He spoke no English, I no Italian. Yet somehow, on the way out, we got into an argument about the relative merits of our respective leaders, Mussolini and Winston Churchill. At the mention of the name 'Churchill', he cried 'No, no, no!' vehemently, then puffed out his chest, jutted his chin and strutted around shouting 'Mussolini!', rather overdoing it, I thought. The next moment, his posture slumped, shoulders sagging, stomach protruding, one hand waving an imaginary cigar, the other pointing to himself as he repeated with an elaborate sneer 'Churchill, Churchill!' Unable to convey in mime the response that there was more to our prime minister than bodybuilding, I conceded defeat with a shrug, adjusted my clothing and left.

But I digress. Absolute power has shown itself, in the behaviour of persons from High Court judges to drill sergeants, bandleaders and schoolmasters, capable of inducing what, to the impartial observer, comes close to insanity. The late Wilfrid Blunt, painter and for over twenty years the Art Master at Eton College, wrote this in his autobiography, *Soft On The Feather* (Michael Russell (Publishing) Ltd, 1986):

> Housemasters at Eton were virtual rulers of their little kingdoms; more like heads of colleges at a university

whose students were boys rather than young men. Thus, though the good housemasters were very good indeed, the few tyrants, fearing nobody, could almost get away with murder.

Wilfrid Blunt came into Eton from outside and took a more dramatic view of the disciplinary life than I, who was born there and had got used to it by the time it affected me directly. Where he was appalled, I tend to recall with amusement the plentiful examples of the destabilising effect that absolute power can have on those who wield it. I'll focus on just one, the man designated by Wilfrid Blunt as an 'unsuppressed sadist', and by one of his pupils, the philosopher A J (Freddy) Ayer, as 'a sadist and a repressed homosexual'.

H K Marsden was known to the boys as 'Bloody Bill'. He was not my housemaster and I was only taught by him for a short period, but I have a vivid memory of one exchange which typified his method. The subject of the lesson was maths, and my efforts to solve a mathematical problem had reached an *impasse*. In Blunt's words, 'a tall, gangling man with a weary, drooping moustache, the remainder of whose face looked as though it had been gone over two days before with a Flymo', Marsden walked over from his desk to stand over me and asked, 'What is 83 by 208 divided by 17 to the power of 3?' or some such gobbledegook, which he had chalked up on the blackboard. He waited, twitching all over with suppressed anger, for an answer that never came. He repeated the question in a now strangulated voice, with the same result. Then, closing his eyes and with a long-suffering sigh, he took us back to basics. 'What is one?' If the first question had sent my brain reeling, this one flattened it with its elusive simplicity, so I could only say 'I don't know, sir', whereupon he lashed out. It wasn't just knuckles with Bloody Bill. He wore a large gold signet ring that assumed the role of a knuckle-duster and took a divot out of the victim's head.

Both Blunt and Ayer recalled H K Marsden with undisguised hatred. I drew a caricature of him at the time which shows no trace of vitriol, so it's clear that, with me, the assault went no further than skin deep. Some aspects of his behaviour as a housemaster were perhaps more sinister, yet paradoxically he was extremely popular with most of the boys in his house. My father, kept on after his retirement as a housemaster until younger 'beaks' returned from the war, willingly accepted his hospitality, his only complaint being that it didn't extend to lighting more than a two-bar gas-fire in the hearth during the freezing winter, a circumstance which I chronicled with another drawing.

In one further story about the misanthropic and misogynistic Marsden, even Wilfrid Blunt hints at a grudging admiration for the old curmudgeon:

> A boy in his house returned late from dining at Windsor Castle and asked his host whether he would be kind enough to give him a line of excuse to his housemaster. The King (George VI) graciously wrote a brief word of apology. Marsden read it, observed that the chap hadn't even bothered to date it, crumpled it up and threw it in the waste-paper basket.

PS: When my father died in 1962, he was buried in the little church in the village of Grundisburgh, near Ipswich, whither my parents had moved after his retirement from Eton. As relatives and friends assembled on the green outside the church, I saw a gaunt figure standing alone some distance away. It was Bloody Bill, who had made the journey to Suffolk to pay his respects. Characteristically, he vanished after the service without at any time saying a word to anyone. It was rather sad.

In the habit of administering *ad hoc* corporal punishment, Bloody Bill was not alone. Another enthusiastic whacker was the puce and pear-shaped Timothy Huson, who likewise targeted the head with what he jovially referred to as 'love taps'. With his wry sense of humour he was generally regarded as a good egg. The fact is, we took in our stride minor assaults upon the person that today would keep the tabloid press in a lather of indignation for weeks and inflate the already bursting coffers of the legal profession. I feel some heavy pronouncement on the subject of ritual corporal punishment coming on, so here is a reminiscence to restore a bit of balance. It's a reproof that I treasure.

At Eton, I was taught what little schoolboy French I know by a benignly eccentric master, Monty Evans. He was born, we all believed, of Franco-Welsh parentage, a mixture that guarantees a high degree of theatricality. I remember him as a handsome man with grey hair brushed in wings above his ears to give an air of flamboyant distinction. The academic gown, a garment that drooped limply from the shoulders of most colleagues, positively billowed when he swept into the classroom. One day he was going from desk to desk, returning work that he had marked overnight – praising some, criticising others in varying degree, always in an extravagant turn of phrase. When he reached my desk, he stood for a moment in dramatic silence, then spoke. 'Lyttelton,' he said in a voice resonant with doom, 'if this was Russia, you would be found in the river in the morning, headless and flo–o–o–oating downstream.'

*

I was brought up, almost from the cradle, with the belief that corporal punishment of one kind or another was 'all part of life's rich pageant'.

(I borrow those words from the late Arthur Marshall, himself a schoolmaster at Oundle and, later, the plump, giggling team-captain opposite Frank Muir on the TV panel show *Call My Bluff.* For a short time, while still teaching, he made some recordings involving what used to be called 'female impersonation'. Starting as a party piece to entertain friends, his hearty schoolmistress, inspired by the girls'-school novels of Angela Brazil, became a national figure. My father loved those records, revelling in such phrases as, on a nature outing, 'Oh dear, Myrtle's turned turtle and crushed her cocoon,' and in the chemistry lab, 'Hmmm, yes – that's enough marsh gas, Mona,' all uttered in a plummy falsetto. 'We're molecules, dear, hurled hugger-mugger into life's foaming crucible,' was a variation of the 'rich pageant' phrase that side-tracked me into this lengthy parenthesis.)

Corporal punishment was not practised by either of my parents, though my father did once aim a kick at my backside when I and others who were expected to know better kept one of my young sisters out late at a funfair in Harlech, causing my mother great anxiety. From as far back as I can remember, he suffered from Paget's disease, an enlargement of the bones. It caused him to list heavily to one side with a limp that, as others observed, was curiously graceful for a man of his large build. The kick was therefore symbolic, missing its target and coming close to giving literal meaning to the cliché, 'This will hurt me more than it hurts you.' When I say that corporal punishment was not practised by my parents, it is no more than the truth. They delegated it. And that's a cue to bring onstage for a brief cameo appearance the redoubtable Nanny Viggers.

My sisters and I grew up under the rule of a succession of nannies. Though I do dimly recall a predecessor called Nanny Gosling, it was Nanny Viggers who played the major part in my early upbringing. (Nannies, as they exist in my memory, had no first names, being known, like army sergeants, solely by their rank. It was a surprise when many years later, after I had mentioned Nanny Viggers on a broadcast, I received a letter from a listener who declared herself to be her niece and referred to her as 'my Auntie Louisa'. (As a child, and indeed through life until that letter arrived, I had no notion that she had any first name other than Nanny (let alone Louisa), nor that she could possibly be anyone's auntie.)

I remember Nanny Viggers as a small woman of indeterminate

age, shaped like a cottage loaf with a stern coiffure similar to that of our present monarch. Rolled over a velvet pad in the front and with a 'bun' at its apex, it seemed to echo the cottage loaf motif. Strict but kindly, she would take us into her bedroom if we were ill or frightened at night. On one such occasion I caught a glimpse, shocking at the time, of her sitting at her dressing table, preparing for bed, with that seemingly indestructible edifice straggling over her shoulders in a chaos of hairpins and curlers.

I have no reason to suppose that Nanny Viggers was anything but a benign influence on her charges, and we were all distressed when the time came for her to move on. But it was she who instilled in me the belief, long since rejected, that corporal punishment was as normal a part of life as eating or sleeping. Even in the nursery it had its ritual, for she was not one for the casual slap. Her chosen weapon, with which we would be threatened or chastised if we were unruly, was the Slipper (I give it the capital initial to bring it in line with the Stocks and the Guillotine). As I recall, it was more of a house-shoe with a hard sole – it certainly felt like it. I was ushered more than once into the bathroom to be, as the euphemistic and misleading saying went, 'given the Slipper'. Thus was established in my head the notion that the Creator, ever a stickler for detail, had designed the human backside to be, among other functions, the normal target of retribution.

That was my introduction to ritual corporal punishment. The spontaneous violence such as that used by the likes of Bloody Bill and Timothy Huson was extracurricular. Built into the system at Eton in the thirties were birchings and canings. The former were administered on rare occasions by either the Headmaster or the Lower Master (head of the lower school) for offences calling for punishment just short of outright expulsion. The canings were delegated by housemasters to the senior boy, or captain, of the house. These canings were at the apex, so to speak, of the fagging system, whereby the most junior boys were, for a while, at the beck and call of the most senior.

At one time, I was allocated as fag to Peter Carrington. Later, as Lord Carrington, he became Foreign Secretary in the pre-Falklands era, resigning when his tolerance, wisdom and impish sense of humour, all expressed in a languid aristocratic drawl, put him at odds with Mrs Thatcher, who regarded those attributes collectively as 'wet'. I met him again in 2005 on *Breakfast With Frost*, the now-defunct BBC TV show hosted by David Frost. After a lapse of sixty-five years during which we went our very separate ways, I was delighted to find him unchanged from the benign fag-master of my memory.

We had a giggling reunion in the green room at the BBC TV Centre, and I regretted that we were not teamed in the subsequent show as a double act, instead of delivering separate and, in my case, well-worn recollections of VE Day. The only thing that disappointed me was that he stoutly denied that I had ever been his fag at Eton. With the greatest respect I back my memory against his. I have always attributed my exceptional prowess in the art of scrambling eggs to the experience of making his supper.

At this point, I feel I owe it to my readers to outline my current recipe for scrambled egg that, with the advance of domestic science and technology, has now reached the peak of refinement.

Ingredients

Two or three eggs, depending on how concerned you are about your cholesterol.

Milk.

Smoked salmon, if you live in the southern half of England where it is not regarded as a symptom of elitism, snobbery or decadence. (I once asked for it in a small supermarket in Crosby, Lancs. The shop assistant's response, a high-pitched shriek of disbelief and derision, attracted a small crowd of shoppers and some passers-by who dashed in from the street thinking that some free professional entertainment had been laid on.)

Pepper.

Garlic Salt.

Tarragon.

The Method
Break the eggs into a bowl, which must be deep enough to avoid splashing. Add a dollop of milk. Using a fork (or one of those ingenious wire gadgets, if you can find it in the chaos of your kitchen drawer), whisk the mixture enthusiastically until it has blended to the colour and consistency of anaemic custard. Add a generous sprinkling of dried tarragon, and pepper and salt to taste. Whisk again with the manic vigour of one who senses that something rather hazardous is about to take place.

Put the bowl into the microwave and set it at three minutes on full power. Start the microwave, but do not go off to watch a bit of television till it bleeps. You will only get involved in a gripping episode of *The Bill* and return, fifty minutes later, to find that you have made something black and crumbling that will offer no pleasing visual contrast to the slice of toast that you are going to burn later. Stay by the microwave and, when you begin to feel a bit edgy, open the door and peer into the bowl. Microwave ovens rather pride themselves on being unpredictable, so you must repeat this inspection at frequent intervals, ignoring the urgent warnings of friends who still believe that if you expose your hands too often to the electro-magnetic waves, your fingers will drop off. They may, but not for sixty years, when most of us are past caring.

The principle of the M-wave (let's start using trendy abbreviations – everybody else does) is that it cooks from the outside inward. Thus, before your very eyes the egg mixture will soon start to show some creeping solidification round the rim of the bowl, leaving a liquid lake in the middle. And this is where the process demands acute concentration. With each inspection, the lake will be seen to have shrunk. It is important not to allow it to disappear altogether – if that happens the egg will have overcooked and fragmented into bits that will bounce about uncontrollably on the toast, evading capture like so many hyperactive grasshoppers on amphetamines. (If we never get around to actually scrambling the egg, we're learning the heck of a lot about biophysics on the journey.)

At some stage round about now, you should tip the chopped smoked salmon into the mix so that it will not have long enough to cook, but can be evenly dispersed when we come to agitate or, as we say, 'scramble' the egg. But I've forgotten to tell you about the chopping bit, and things are moving so fast that it's too late to do so now. So, quickly smooth back the cover that you have ripped off the pack of smoked salmon, replace the fish and put the whole caboodle back in the fridge for another occasion. That way, you will avoid finding yourself, when you come to eat the egg, chewing on the squares of invisible plastic film that separate the salmon slices. By the time all that's done, the lake, as I have described it, will have dwindled to the size of, say, a two-pound coin. Quickly remove the bowl from the microwave, go at it with a fork like one possessed, blending the still-liquid egg with the rest. When the mixture is poured on to the slice of toast, it will look soft, shiny and appetising.

I have assumed that the reader who has got thus far will have known how to make the slice of toast; if not, a few words of advice. Few households nowadays have the sort of roaring open fire before which one used to be able to toast the bread on a fork, achieving a wonderful golden-brown finish that spread evenly over the slice and up the hand, wrist and forearm as far as the elbow. Nowadays the popular alternative is the electric toaster, which is indeed a boon. But be sure the machine is fully run-in before use.

If not, it is likely to fling the finished slice up to the ceiling and thence into some distant corner of the room, where it will be pounced upon and devoured by a dog, a cat or even perhaps a swan that has entered the house unannounced. Swans will eat anything, which is why I hope you haven't thrown away those charred remains of the overcooked egg. *Bon Appetit!*

Chairman Humph, in Ainsley Harriott mode

Now, if I describe the details of the Eton fagging procedure in the thirties in too much detail, it will be assumed that I have strayed into the realms of wild fantasy, where Ossa and Pelion jostle for supremacy. (The talk of 'fags' may mislead American readers even more, but I can't help that. We're talking history here, not semantics.) In the hierarchy of a house, the very senior boys were members of the 'Library', a sort of common room with privileges attached. The very junior boys belonged to a pool of 'fags' who, as well as serving a specific 'fag-master', could be summoned at any time of the day by a member of the Library to run random errands.

All the senior boy had to do was go out into a corridor and shout, 'BOY!!!' at the top of his voice, usually more than once and with the syllable prolonged. Every 'fag' within earshot would have to drop whatever he was doing and scamper in the direction of the voice. The last one to arrive would then be ordered to perform the required errand, whether it was taking an essay to a master's house or picking up a bag of doughnuts from Rowland's, the school 'tuck shop'. The official justification for this primitive rite was that it was a great 'leveller', as every boy, whether the son of a duke or a dustman, had to go through it. Leaving aside the low statistical rating of dustmen among Eton parents, it has been my observation that dukes, even royalty, who were cut down to size by the process, have had little difficulty in reverting, within a few short years, to the manner to which they were born.

I know this is sounding crazier with every sentence but I can't help it, so let the *farrago* continue.

There was one period in the day – after supper, I recall – when the procedure took a more sinister turn, and the cry of 'BO–O–O–O–O–OY!' would set butterflies flapping frenetically in the stomach of every junior boy who heard it. At that time of day, it signified that the errand would be to fetch a miscreant to the Library for a brief reprimand and a swift caning, usually consisting of what was euphemistically termed 'six of the best'. The offences that attracted this retribution were usually quite trivial – the noisy mayhem termed 'ragging' being the commonest. I was caned twice. I won't linger on the first occasion since it involved a house-captain who was clearly a candidate for psychiatric treatment. Charging across the room and grunting loudly with every blow in a way now familiar at Wimbledon during a hard-fought match, he eventually drew blood. I squealed loudly under the assault but, boy, was I proud of those weals afterwards!

The second episode was altogether more civilised, the wielder of the cane being a shy, soft-spoken and, on the occasion, seemingly reluctant house-captain called George Mann, who subsequently became nationally known as captain of the English cricket team. Years later, when I was in a theatre foyer signing my recordings, he came up to the table with his wife who, before we had a chance to renew our acquaintance, said in a voice loud enough to encompass the whole room, 'D'you remember my husband George? I believe he beat you at school!'

There is no limit to the average upper-class female's capacity to embarrass her menfolk in public!

Chairman Humph in mysogynistic mode

Since I am the very personification of fair-mindedness, I will balance that comment with a recent memory that encapsulates the principle of Womens' Lib. The scene is the Brent Cross Shopping

Centre in Hendon. A woman and her small daughter are standing
in the spot on the upper floor designated as a meeting place. The
daughter appears distressed.

Daughter: 'Oh, Mummy, we're lost!'

Mother: 'No, we're not, darling, we're here. It's Daddy who's lost.'

Apropos caning, I was once interviewed on the erstwhile BBC
TV *Breakfast Show* by Selena Scott, a lady of beauty and charm
but not spectacular powers of comprehension. I told her that, at
Eton, it was discovered that the best way to protect one's person
in the event of a caning was to go down the road to Rowland's and
buy several large slices of cooked ham. She looked puzzled. 'You
mean, as a bribe?' When I told her that it was actually to stuff
hastily down the back of one's trousers if and when a summons to
the Library occurred, she hurried on to the next question. There
was, in fact, method in the madness, it having been scientifically
established in the Laboratory of Hard Knocks that the thwack of
cane on buttock could be simulated better by ham, with its animal
affiliations, than by an exercise book or stiff-backed envelope.

*

It's time to move on, and not a moment too soon, if you ask me.
My time doing military service in World War II offered much
opportunity to confirm Lord Acton's dictum on power. A lot of it
was spent on parade grounds – as a recruit, officer cadet and
eventually, a Guards officer at the same Caterham depot where I
had suffered my own initiation. In each capacity, I had the
opportunity to study in the field that fascinating but dangerously
unstable species, the drill sergeant. It is not strictly true to say that
on the barrack square, drill sergeants had absolute power. Indeed,
my function as an officer – when I strolled about during parades
with a stick under my arm, looking lofty but wrapped in my own
thoughts – was to deter them from excess. But their remit was so
broad, stopping just short of grievous bodily harm or murder, that
they were, in fact, dictators on the tarmac.

One clear sign that drill sergeants were becoming unhinged was the eccentric way in which they uttered the words of command. Regimental Sergeant-Major Britton, who was the major-domo among drill sergeants when I was at Sandhurst Military College in the early forties, became quite famous for the power of his voice on parade. After retirement, he was often booked to appear on television programmes, shouting. When, on a mass parade, he called the assembled squads to attention with the command 'Parade . . . 'Shun!' he lingered tantalisingly on the first word and then, after a pause, uttered the second in a piercing altissimo shriek that loosened the putty on the windows of the main building and brought birds thudding, stunned, from the trees.

The resourcefulness of drill sergeants in pursuit of absolute power over their victims was, in my experience, limitless. There is no need here to recall those tyrants whose methods, often obscene, crossed the boundary of zeal into overt sadism. There was plenty of creative humour about. I recall a wry Glaswegian who, if a rival squad was in the vicinity, would halt us, stand us at ease and invite us to watch as they passed. This short dialogue would ensue:

> Sergeant, derisively: 'Look at 'em! Turrible, aren't they?' Squad, mumbling and stumbling into an ambush: 'Yes, Sar'nt.' Sergeant, rounding on us: 'WELL, THEY'RE A DARM SIGHT BETTER THAN YEW HEAP!!!'

A nuisance examined. (See p.83)

It Just Occurred to Me . . .

At Sandhurst, at any given time of the day, the large barrack square was alive with the diverse movement of squads stamping, marching or jogging in all directions. During these parades, the adjutant would often appear on a horse, to saunter about looking authoritative. Periodically, the horse would lift its tail and casually deposit on the tarmac, while still on the move, what in the rules of golf is designated as a 'loose hazard'. One sergeant who, for a while, controlled my destiny, seized these events to galvanise his recalcitrant squad into action, steering us at the double over the steaming pile and back again while gleefully reciting our shortcomings.

One of the less eminent NCOs whose challenge it was to turn me from a recruit into an automaton was, off duty, what one would describe as a 'pussycat' – soft-spoken, gentle and humorous. It was all the more alarming therefore when, having patiently demonstrated to us the intricate rifle-slapping and foot-stamping routine of presenting arms, he would first ask us, in a voice of sweet reasonableness, 'Do you understand?' and then, in response to our mumbled 'Yes, Sar'nt,' suddenly take leave of his senses. Making a meal of every word, he repeated the question at the top of his voice – 'DO . . . YOU. . . . UNDERSTAND?' shuffling his feet so fast with the effort that his hat flew off and he briefly levitated.

*

One might think that jazz music, born of rebellion and iconoclasm, would prove a safe haven from the corrupting influence of power. It might have been so but for the arrival of the phenomenon later dubbed the Swing Era. A flavour of that period can be gleaned from this observation by Whitney Balliett, for many years jazz columnist, and another erstwhile star in the *New Yorker*, who wrote about the drummer Gene Krupa:

> Short, handsome, dark-haired, and smiling, he established the image of the drummer as madman. It was an image – calculated or not – that hypnotised the eye and stopped the

29

ears. When he played, his hair fell over his eyes; he chewed gum; he hunched over his drums or reared back, arms straight in the air, like a politician at a rally; he sweated; in his climactic moments he converted his arms and hands and drumsticks into sculptured blurs. The mania for speed had begun to take hold in the late thirties, and Krupa was its epitome.

That observation might well have seen the word 'mania' used for the very first time in music criticism. It was not out of place. Though not on such a global scale as 'Beatlemania' in the sixties, the adulation accorded to the leaders of the big Swing orchestras came to attract the same manic fervour.

The French do not call the modern multi-functional drum kit *la batterie* for nothing. Krupa, flailing about on a rostrum above the rest of the band, became a star to the Swing Era's youthful following. He took full advantage of the power that the adulation bestowed and in the process went, to Mr Balliett's critical eye, seemingly bonkers. But when Whitney Balliett wrote those words, Krupa was a member of Benny Goodman's orchestra and, as such, did not wield absolute power. That resided in his eccentric bandleader.

Benny Goodman, like most of the bandleaders in those heady days, had started his career in the late twenties as 'one of the boys' in a group of young musicians bitten by the jazz bug. The birth of the Swing Band, through a marriage of big commercial dancebands and small, improvising jazz groups, converted the most business-orientated of these enthusiasts into all-powerful dictators, holding, in an insecure and fickle profession, economic as well as musical power. Anecdotes abound, mostly from those who worked with him, concerning Benny Goodman's increasingly eccentric methods of maintaining his power.

Tenor saxophonist Zoot Sims was once asked, in the sixties, what it was like touring in Communist Russia with the Goodman band. His answer was, 'When you're with Benny Goodman, every day is like touring in Russia.'

In the mid-thirties, the Paramount Theatre in New York was foremost among cinemas in booking the big Swing attractions to play four or five sets a day in between the movies. When the practice started in the late thirties, Swing was the thing and the bands came to outstrip the feature films as an attraction. To simplify the logistics of getting a band on and off stage, the Paramount installed a rising orchestra pit on which the band, fully set up, would rise like Botticelli's Venus to the rowdy acclaim of young audiences. The system was still in force in 1945, when Benny Goodman was booked after a long absence. The band was then on the wane, and Goodman's eccentricity was rising correspondingly. Baritone saxist Danny Banks was a member:

'We had to sit on hard stools for four or five shows a day, which made it awfully tough on your rear end. My friend Al Epstein, a darling guy who played tenor in the band, had bleeding piles, and to get some relief, he went into the drug store and bought an inflatable rubber ring to use as a cushion. Well, Benny came out to the pit early while the coming attractions were still on, and he saw this thing on top of Epstein's stool. It wasn't orderly – everybody had a white-painted stool and there's this one red rubber ring – so Benny reached into his pocket, pulled out a safety-pin and punctured a hole in it. When Epstein sat down and the ring collapsed, he realised that there had been some foul play, so after the show, he bought a tyre repair kit and patched it up. But Benny still had the safety pin and punctured it again. And it went on that way until Epstein ran out of patches. Benny never said a word to him about it. I think he saw it as a game.'

Described in *Swing, Swing, Swing: The Life and Times of Benny Goodman* by Ross Fierstone (Hodder & Stoughton, 1993)

Bandleader and trombonist Tommy Dorsey was, during the Swing Era, one of Benny Goodman's chief rivals – and not only in the realms of musical prowess. One of his musicians recalled an incident involving that most polite and gentle of men, clarinettist Buddy de Franco:

> Tommy insisted that the soloists played the solos note for note as on the records. One night, fed up, Buddy changed the clarinet solo on 'Opus One'. Tommy lunged after him off stage and demanded to know what he thought he had been doing. 'It's not artistic to play the same solo every night, Tommy,' said Buddy. Dorsey exploded. 'Artistic? Artistic? Who d' you think you are, you stale shit-heel? Art Tatum? Go and be artistic on somebody else's band. You're fired.'

These stories were passed on to me through the grapevine by my good friend, the jazz writer and, for a long time, broadcaster Steve Voce. The first time he was with Dorsey, Buddy de Franco got fed up with being on the road and decided to leave the band. De Franco recalled:

> I'd made a few connections in Los Angeles. André Previn was making a film in which Kieron Moore played a clarinet player. I was to teach him fingering and dub the soundtrack. I'd got a few club dates lined up. So I went to Tommy and told him I wanted to leave. Now, you don't leave Tommy.
> 'Where are you going?' Dorsey demanded.
> 'I've got a few gigs lined up in Los Angeles,' I told him.
> 'You ain't got nothing. You leave my band, you don't work,' said Tommy. I left. Suddenly the club dates vanished. I asked André about the film and he said the job had evaporated. Apart from a couple of Sunday afternoon jam sessions, I didn't work for eighteen months. At the end of that time Tommy phoned me. 'You got enough wrinkles

in your bag?' he asked (like 'stale shit-heel', another of his fanciful expressions).

Steve Voce's informant takes up the story:

> Although he was broke and had no work, Buddy said 'I'm doing real good. I've got plenty of regular work.' Tommy brushed this aside.
>
> 'What the hell, we need a clarinet player in this band. Will you come back?' Buddy stipulated what he wanted paying and particularly mentioned 'everything extra', which meant all travelling expenses. If you didn't mention that at the outset, you didn't get them. Dorsey said, 'OK, you got it and everything extra.'
>
> 'Then wire me a thousand dollars right away,' said Buddy. Dorsey whooped with triumph.
>
> 'You're broke! You stale shit-heel, I knew it! You're broke!'
>
> But he wired Buddy the money and Buddy rejoined the band.

The nickname 'Buddy' is ubiquitous in jazz and can give misleading information as to the character of its recipient. I have described Buddy de Franco as 'polite and gentle'. As a bandleader, the virtuoso drummer Buddy Rich was neither polite nor gentle. Tales of his irascibility multiplied as he grew older. This is a story told to me and others by the American drummer, Jake Hanna. I have put it in my own words from memory.

The band was once booked into a small Midwest club, not blessed with state-of-the-art equipment. Buddy Rich arrived a day early to look over the place and state his requirements. The show was to start with the room pitch-black, except for a pin-spot focussed on a black curtain in front of the bandstand. A voice would announce, 'Now, ladies and gentlemen, we proudly present the world's greatest drummer, Mr BUDDY RICH!', at which point the tiny spot would expand and the curtain would part to reveal Mr Rich seated behind his impressive array of drums and cymbals on a rostrum in the middle of his band.

Now, the club had no curtain, no spotlight, no rostrum and no facility for suddenly damping all the lights. However, frantic activity by the management procured them all, after a fashion, in time for the opening, including a black sheet to act as a makeshift curtain. Prior information about the elaborate routine did not, for some reason, reach Sam Most, a saxophonist in the band. He was seated at the small bar, chatting to a customer and ready to go on stage at the last minute, as musicians do, when the room was suddenly plunged into darkness and the booming voice started to make the opening announcement.

With scant knowledge of the room's geography, Sam Most made a panic-stricken dash for the stage, blundering into tables and knocking over customers. He got there, but tripped on an unforeseen step. For support, he grabbed the first thing that came to hand, which happened to be the black curtain. Parting company with its hastily assembled and fragile fittings, this collapsed on to the stage, engulfing the world's greatest drummer. Simultaneously, the pin-spot expanded, to reveal an amorphous black heap in mid-stage from which, after a pregnant pause, came a muffled shout: 'WHOEVER YOU ARE, YOU'RE FIRED!!'

Glenn Miller was by nature a strict disciplinarian. The tenor saxophonist Tex Beneke, who served with Miller in both his civilian and Army band, bore witness in an interview:

> Glenn was strict. Everybody knew that. He was tough on musicians, all right. He used to insist on proper haircuts, proper shines, both feet on the floor and the same amount of white showing in every man's breast-pocket handkerchief.

When, at his own request, Miller enlisted in the US Army to revolutionise its military music, his promotion to the rank of Major in charge of the Army Air Force Band seemed to lift both his feet off the floor and launch him in the direction of cloud-cuckoo land. In one dictatorial move, he ordered all musicians with moustaches to shave them off. Describing the incident, Miller's biographer, George T Simon wrote, in *Glenn Miller And His Orchestra* (W H Allen):

> For some, who had nursed their growths for years, it became a traumatic experience. And for others, like some brass players, whose very blowing of their instruments had become dependent upon those mustaches (sic), the loss was indeed serious.

Simon concludes:

> . . . of all the moves that Glenn ever made, this always seemed to me to have been the most senseless and least sensitive. According to erstwhile Miller trumpeter Bernie Privin, 'The only explanation he ever gave us was that we looked too much like gangsters.'

I like the 'too much'! Readers wondering what essential role facial hair could possibly play in the production of sound from an instrument should know that, once established, a moustache forms one component of a player's embouchure, a sensitive structure which reacts unfavourably if altered by a fraction of a millimetre. I once wore a moustache, sometimes with or without an accompanying beard. Judging from pictures of me in my wartime Army days, its style was not so much gangster, more Lord Kitchener. When I eventually became more or less clean-shaven, I retained for some years a little vestigial shrub below the lower lip, too small to be flattered by the term 'goatee'. I got rid of it when it became a bore, having to be trimmed regularly to a consistent size so as not to disturb the sacred embouchure.

The population of the world is divided equally between those who are nature's prefects and those who are forever snotty-nosed kids.

Chairman Humph, in demographic mode

I hope and believe that I belong in the second category and that as a disciplinarian I fit into the Duke Ellington model. Apropos leading one of the greatest ever jazz orchestras in the world, Ellington once said, 'No musicians are going to put me in the nuthouse. If we go there, we'll go together – and I'll be driving the coach.' His method of dealing with indiscipline was either to ignore it, or to punish the wrongdoer in a subtle way by, for instance, calling up all his taxing solo features one after the other. I was witness to a striking example of the first method at a concert in Leeds in 1958.

In his programme at the time, Ellington would announce a composition by the high-note specialist William 'Cat' Anderson entitled 'El Gato'. Four of the five trumpeters – Anderson himself, Harold 'Shorty' Baker, Clark Terry and Ray Nance – would come to the front of the stage to play the ensemble theme, a Spanish bull-fight motif, and to take solos in turn. At Leeds, Shorty Baker was still nursing a severe hangover from an all-night party at the Cavern in Liverpool the previous evening and declined to come onstage. The absence of one trumpet threatened to throw the whole orchestration into disarray, so when the Duke began to introduce 'El Gato' in his customary way, the musicians behind him waved and hissed to draw his attention to the empty seat in the trumpet section which he appeared not to have noticed. No one gesticulated and stage-whispered more urgently than the drummer, Sam Woodyard, who was nearest to him. Ellington ploughed on regardless, right up to the point at which he customarily introduced the trumpet players. On this occasion he said, in his most urbane manner, 'Usually, this number features four of our trumpeters,' at which point he turned, looked straight at the empty chair and went on, 'but Sam Woodyard is playing drums tonight.' He then launched the number with a wild cry and an energetic downbeat, leaving the three remaining trumpeters to sort things out for themselves, which of course they did with aplomb.

I can remember only one occasion on which I meted out Ellington-style retribution to one of my musicians.

In 1990, we went for a few days to Hong Kong. Adrian Macintosh, my drummer of long-standing and a valued member of the Lyttelton band 'family', is an inveterate sightseer. It's a wholly admirable trait except when a performance of three one-hour sets is in prospect in the evening. One day, he booked himself and his wife Sheila on a boat excursion round the neighbouring islands, which set off at 6.30 a.m. Before the gig that night, a dance in our hotel, he was full of all the wonderful places they had visited and sights they had seen. I listened with the mounting vindictiveness of one who had spent the day, perhaps wisely but certainly boringly, doing little that involved getting off my hotel bed. By the end of the third set, Adrian was visibly wilting. Our finale at that time was an up-tempo version of the tune 'Avalon', which included a couple of choruses of drum solo, at the end of which he would customarily glance over to me to cue in the final ensemble. That night I signalled for another thirty-two bars – and then another. It was only when I noticed that a sort of living rigor mortis was creeping from his wrists up towards his shoulders that I relented and brought the proceedings to a close. No words were spoken, but since then, the single word 'Avalon' has been enough to induce caution when mountains or nature trails beckon.

PS: There is symmetry to the story. I learned from Adrian much later that the house in which he was born was called Avalon. In 2005, he and Sheila went on holiday in California, untrammelled by any musical responsibilities. One of the excursions advertised was a visit to the island of Avalon. Adrian felt compelled to take it up, in order to complete the circle of coincidence.

There was a certain method in the madness of the dictator bandleaders. As in many other areas of human endeavour, controlling a work force of disparate and often wildly eccentric characters is better done by an acknowledged leader than by a committee, or even shared leadership. I once interviewed the great jazz violinist Stéphane Grappelli in the later years of his life. He was often asked about his erstwhile association, at the head of Le Quintet du Hot Club de France, with the wayward gypsy guitarist Django Reinhardt. Stéphane rated Django as his superior in musical talent but an impossible business partner, but that was the role that Django coveted.

Although a musician for whom the word 'genius' was appropriate, Django Reinhardt could neither read nor write. Nevertheless, when business matters were to be discussed in the office of a promoter or agent, he always insisted on being present. Usually he would sit quietly while Grappelli did all the talking. Once in a while, he felt that, as co-leader, he should make his presence felt. Thus, when a bulky contract was handed across the desk for signature, he would snatch it from Grappelli's hand and make as if to read it diligently clause by clause. At some random point he would select a section and, stabbing at it with a forefinger, pronounce emphatically 'Non! Non, non, non, non, NON!' More often than not, it was the clause stating that the band's food, accommodation and travel would be paid for by the management!

Louis Armstrong was never a baton-waggler. On the odd – and I mean odd – film clips which show him conducting a big band, he is to be seen out front beating the air with both arms simultaneously on the first and third beats of the bar in movements remarkably stilted and awkward for one to whom every other aspect of the music came with such easy grace. He was happiest with a small group, once telling an interviewer proudly, 'When that curtain goes up and you hear "When It's Sleepy Time Down South" (his theme tune), you see me up there blowin'.'

As a disciplinarian, Armstrong was easy-going, having in the mid-thirties handed over to his agent and manager, Joe Glaser, the business of hiring and firing musicians. There exist recordings of his band in rehearsal in which he is heard leading primarily by example, demonstrating what he wanted by playing the passage on his trumpet. However short that passage was, he would blow it with the same energy and passion that he would invest in a finished performance. It would be a very obtuse sideman who failed to get the message.

Outside the music itself, his sternest rules concerned his relationship with his audience. Those who worked under him would often declare that, if the curtain went up on a show to reveal only a handful of customers in the house, their hearts would sink. They knew that he was about to work them twice as hard.

I was once present at a press conference in which Louis Armstrong was asked about the performances which the top bands gave at the Paramount Theatre in the thirties, in between the movie shows. He described how they would start at 10.30 a.m. and go on intermittently through the day till the screenings finished at night. When he said that the curtain would often go up to show no more than three sleepy people in the house, the reporter who raised the subject said, in effect, 'Oh well, at least you could take it easy then.' Armstrong's reply was indignant: 'You don't take it easy, never! One of those guys might have hitch-hiked three hundred miles to hear your band for the first time. He don't do that to see you take it easy!'

Similarly, one of his musicians told me that, one night in a club, the attendance was so low that the owner came backstage before the show to suggest that his staff, the musicians, Louis and, no doubt, he himself could curtail the performance and go home early. The man was asked sternly, 'Did those people out there pay a hundred per cent at the box office?' When the manager nodded and shrugged as if the subject was of no importance, Louis Armstrong came back with, 'Then they get a hundred per cent of the show.'

It has to be said that Louis Armstrong's relaxed attitude to life owed much to a long relationship with what has been known over the years as tea, grass, reefer, muggles, gage, joint, muta, shuzzit, pot and goodness knows what other affectionate nicknames. Ironically, there was a medical dimension to the start of the affair. Though no teetotaller (when he was in London in the mid-fifties, he would, when asked, request what he called B&B, a daunting mix of brandy and Benedictine), Armstrong was always stern about those musicians who ruined their health with alcohol – and there were plenty in his generation. When somebody in an interview mentioned the premature death of the trumpeter Bunny Berigan in 1942 at the age of 34 his first response was, 'He had no business dying that young.'

In a long letter to British jazz writer the late Max Jones, quoted in the biography entitled *Louis* by Max and trumpeter-historian John Chilton, Armstrong described his and his friends' conversion from alcohol to cannabis in terms resembling present-day health freakery.

> Speaking of 1931 – we did call ourselves Vipers, which could have been anybody from all walks of life that smoked and respected gage. That was our cute little name for marijoana (sic), and it was a misdomeanor (sic) in those days. . . . We always looked at pot as a sort of medicine, a cheap drunk and one with much better thoughts than one that's full of liquor . . .

Later in the letter, he described a defining moment in his life:

> I've always been physic minded . . . every time I'd light up with a cat (viper) I'd mention laxatives and was happy to know that everybody got the message . . . Then here comes this book – a health book written by Gaylord Hauser. When I read down to the part where he recommended some herbs – herbal laxatives – I said to myself, 'Hmmm, these herbs reminds of the same as what my mother picked down by the tracks in New Orleans . . .' Right away I went to the Health Store and bought myself a box of Swiss Kriss and took a great big tablespoonful . . . [the prescribed dose being one

teaspoonful, I will leave the result to the reader's imagination] Wow! I said to myself, yessindeed (sic), this is what I need from now on – and forsake all others.'

Few who came into contact with Louis Armstrong in his later life will be unaware of the existence of Swiss Kriss. From the moment he began touring the world as a superstar in the fifties onwards, he appointed himself an unofficial promoter of the substance, bestowing upon friends and acquaintances alike information and, in special instances, free samples. On one European visit, he and his wife Lucille had an audience with the Pope. It would not surprise me to learn that the bejewelled hand that bestowed the Papal blessing withdrew holding, to its owner's surprise, several packets of Swiss Kriss. Had the pontiff taken on board Louis Armstrong's prescription of 'one tablespoonful', the outcome might have shaken the Catholic Church to its foundations.

Duggie Tobutt, a road manager who escorted Louis on a British tour in the sixties, made the mistake of telling his famous charge that he had suffered a heart attack a few years before. He was subjected to a stern pep talk about neglecting his internal plumbing and given a packet of Swiss Kriss to be taken that night in the hotel when he went to bed. Without reading the label to confirm the correct dose, Duggie took a tablespoonful as Louis directed. At noon next day, the phone rang in Louis Armstrong's room. After a certain amount of heavy breathing a voice, hardly daring to raise itself above a whisper, said, 'Duggie here . . . is there any antidote to that stuff?'

Louis Armstrong averred, in his letter to Max Jones, that he gave up smoking marijuana in 1931 after spending nine days in jail on a charge of possession. Indeed, the letter includes a touching open message of farewell:

Mary Warner, honey, you sure was good and I enjoyed you 'heep much'. But the price got a little too high to pay (law wise). At first you was a 'misdomeanor'. But as the years rolled on you lost your misdo and got meanor and meanor . . .

The evidence from many sources is that Louis Armstrong deviated in this matter from his intention to 'tell it like it wuz', that the touching farewell to 'Mary Warner' was, in fact, a short-term *au revoir*, and that the resumed affair continued without loss of ardour until his dying day. I can contribute a small jot of evidence to this.

One day during one of the Armstrong tours in the sixties, I was approached by an emissary from his camp and given an envelope containing three neatly rolled cigarettes, with a request to pass them on to Max Jones, who was known to be a friend of mine.

Skidmore.

I was no stranger to 'pot', having been persuaded years before to sample it by fellow musician, Jimmy Skidmore, of whom I have written affectionately elsewhere in this book. Jimmy was so persistent in his efforts to enrol me in the club that, in a hotel on tour, I agreed, though nervous of a step into the unknown that might send me careering into the hotel corridors out of control and laughing uproariously.

It was not an auspicious initiation. In his hotel room, he produced a matchbox that appeared to contain, at first sight, some sort of squashed insect. It turned out to be a 'roach' (I was not ignorant of the jargon) – a damp, dark brown fag-end which he removed with the reverent care of a priest dispensing a sacred wafer at Communion.

Seeing that I was threatening to throw up at the sight of it, he volunteered to demonstrate the technique that would transport me into Elysium. The problem was, that having lit up and inhaled deeply, he was overtaken by a fit of coughing. The sight of him heaving with cheeks blown out, lips tight shut and eyes popping, desperately trying to retain the precious smoke while a barrage of bronchial spasms threatened to release it prematurely, seemed to confirm my direst forebodings. But I took my turn like a man. The result was total anticlimax. Apart from an instant sore throat and a slight light-headedness probably caused by hyper-ventilation, I experienced nothing.

However, when I received the package intended for Max Jones, I was unable to resist the temptation to try again with one of the more promising 'joints'. Again the result was negative, so I put the rest in a drawer along with the dozen or so unopened packets of Swiss Kriss that I had acquired after several encounters with the Master. Months later, when it was too late to pass them on to Max, I took them outside and burnt them in the incinerator. For several hours, the squirrels in my garden looked euphoric, so I must have missed something.

P.S., told to me at some time along the way:

When Louis Armstrong toured in the latter years of his life, his entourage included one Doc Pugh, who was designated his 'valet', though the modern term 'gopher' (go for) is more accurate. One of Doc's many and varied functions was to marshal and assist the stream of fans who would find their way backstage to see their idol. As such he made many friends of all nationalities. One was a young fan in Germany who never missed an Armstrong visit. An occasion arose when he turned up backstage to find no Doc Pugh to greet him. He got in to see Louis nonetheless, and asked him, 'Vere iss Doc Pugh?' to be told, 'He died two months ago.' Shocked, the young man – whose mastery of English grammar had not progressed beyond the present tense – asked, 'But vot iss wrong viss him?' Louis Armstrong replied genially, 'When you're dead, pretty well everything's wrong with you!'

I can't take the spotlight off the idiosyncrasies of big bandleaders without a word of sympathy. Unlike army sergeants, they are not presented with nervous and pliable recruits to deal with. To pursue the analogy, most of the sidemen in the big dance or swing bands were, and still are, 'old soldiers' of a rebellious or hard-bitten nature.

> The trombonist Bill Harris, for some years a star of the Woody Herman Orchestra, was an inveterate practical joker. The orchestra was once booked to do a stage show that involved dancers who, at a certain point, made their entrance down a wide ramp that effectively split the band down the middle. Finding himself seated right next to the ramp, Harris was presented with irresistible temptation. The show ran for several nights. By the time it came to the final night, Bill Harris had equipped himself with one of those wooden toy ducks with loose legs that enable it to waddle down a slope.
>
> In every show, Woody Herman would play his own special feature, a slow, sentimental ballad on alto saxophone. On this night, when the solo reached its most sensitive moment, Bill put the duck on the slope and gave it a gentle shove. It duly waddled into the spotlight, quacking loudly.
>
> Another story told to me by Steve Voce

In my experience, which has involved leading a big band on limited occasions, some of the hardest men in the business are trumpet players. It's not hard to understand. Those who do 'sessions' – for recording, broadcasting or in theatre pits – spend much of their working lives banging themselves in the mouth with a chunk of brass, a practice not conducive to patience or docility.

The renowned British dance-band leader, Geraldo – né Gerald Bright – had a long-running band show on BBC radio. He signed off at the end, in his somewhat lugubrious voice, with the words, 'Well, the clock on the wall says "Geraldo, that's all."' One night, inevitably, he mistakenly spoonerised it. He got as far as, 'Well, the wall on the clock says "Geraldo . . ."' when a voice loud enough for the entire listening nation to hear called out from the trumpet section '. . . You schmock!'

*

To those with ambitions to stand on a rostrum, balcony or barrack square ordering the rest of us about in grandiose fashion, I commend this thought:

> As we journey through life, discarding baggage along the way, we should keep an iron grip, to the very end, on the capacity for silliness. It preserves the soul from desiccation.

> Chairman Humph in introspective mode

It was in March 2001 that my band and Elkie Brooks, a dear friend and occasional musical colleague of many years standing, recorded an album together devoted to the Blues – of which she is, to me, the best exponent outside of America, and superior to quite a few inside. Having achieved fourteen successful tracks in two-and-a-half days, we assembled in the hotel where the band was staying for a celebratory dinner.

The mood was one of euphoria bordering on hysteria. In the middle of much laughter and joking, Elkie turned to me and said, 'You know, you can be quite silly at times.' I accepted the comment gratefully in the spirit in which it was given, as a compliment. In this elevated context, we are not talking about 'silly' as synonymous with 'stupid', 'fatuous' or 'inane'. Of all the options offered by the *Concise Oxford Dictionary*, perhaps 'innocent' comes nearest. It's that ability to regress temporarily to that period in childhood when one did or said things spontaneously, solely for the fun they produced. As this book unfolds, I am becoming more and more aware that the part of my brain that involves memory is just one vast repository of silliness. On the whole, I am quite pleased about this. It has enabled me to look back with some equanimity over a life that has had its fair share of downs as well as ups. The redeeming quality of silliness should not be scorned.

For all I know, both sets of 'famous last words' attributed to King George V may belong in the realms of myth. 'How goes it with the Empire?' always seemed to me an improbable and, if true, sententious line on which to expend his last remaining breath. I prefer to believe, as evidence of the survival of silliness to the end, his reported reply to his wife Queen Mary's assurance that, on his recovery, they would go once again to Bognor for his convalescence. 'Bugger Bognor!' has the true ring of silliness, suggesting that he may have shuffled off this mortal coil chuckling to himself.

My father died on 1 May 1962, so this letter, dictated to my mother, could well stand as his official last words. They are, indeed, intensely moving, not least in the evidence that, even *in extremis,* his feel for the literary phrase didn't desert him.

Grundisburgh

25 April 1962

There is nothing in anything except my gratitude and the wonderfulness of Pamela (she mustn't cross that out). So what then? I am not even a chaos – I am a vast infinity. She will write you any more, if there is anything. Love to Ruth and bless you both. Oh the boredom!

A letter to Rupert Hart-Davis, the last entry in the six-volume *Lyttelton–Hart-Davis Letters* (published by John Murray)

I have some alternative last words to set beside it.

When my father became terminally ill with liver cancer, my mother's sisters rallied to her support. Sibell (Fulford) came to stay in the house, and my Aunt Madeline (Wigan), who lived not far away in Suffolk, visited regularly. It was she who, to give practical help, put at my mother's disposal the services of a lady known affectionately as Buffy. She was one of those erstwhile retainers, not unusual in big country houses, who had stayed on in their own accommodation to become virtually a member of the family.

One day, near the end, Buffy was busying herself around the ground-floor room to which my father had been moved. He had never, in life, welcomed fuss of any sort – his study had for decades resisted the invasion of anyone carrying so much as a feather duster with intent to tidy it. But since he had reached the stage of slipping in and out of consciousness, it was thought that he would barely notice the presence in the room of anyone but my mother, who was constantly at his bedside. I cannot tell it first-hand, since Sibell urged me and my sisters not to go in and see him. He would not have been aware of it and my mother's presence was enough. So it was from Sibell that I learned that, as Buffy bustled about her business, he tried to speak. When my mother leant close to hear the painfully whispered words, they were, 'Tell Buffy to get her vast bum out of here.'

This seems an appropriate place to record that I was born on 23 May 1921, a birthday shared by bandleader Artie Shaw and actress Joan Collins, a fact to which I can attach no significance at all, since I have no belief in horoscopes or star-signs. So I don't really know why I've raised the subject, except as an excuse to put my first reported words on the record.

I was told, and sometimes I imagine I can vaguely remember it, that I was with my father at a bus stop in front of a row of houses when a cat came out of a garden gate and walked lazily towards us, no doubt with the friendliest of intentions. Peering apprehensively from behind my father's leg, which must have seemed to me like a tree-trunk at that age, I uttered words that I will enshrine here as a precocious example of wisdom and perception:

Let's dead that cat before it eats us!

The first recorded words of Chairman Humph, circa 1923

Eighty-three years later, I still regard that as good advice, though I would perhaps word it differently. It's never wise to trust a cat. My wife Jill used to adopt them in large numbers. One visitor showed such aggressive tendencies that it had to stay in a box in the courtyard, from which point it terrorised all comers. Twice in one day I had to rush the double-glazing man from Thermastore down to Accident and Emergency in Barnet Hospital. If things had turned out for the worst, his last words would have been, 'Don't worry – cats like me.'

The difference between an exhibitionist and an eccentric is that the exhibitionist demands an audience; the eccentric is oblivious to it.

Chairman Humph, probably in eccentric mode

It's fortunate that I was no stranger to eccentricity when, in 1953, Bruce Turner joined my band on alto saxophone and clarinet. It's difficult to explain to those unacquainted with the internal politics of post-war British jazz just what a furore his arrival caused. A deep schism existed between the Revivalists (later revised to Traditionalists), who favoured a reconstruction of the New Orleans-style jazz recorded in the twenties, and the Modernists, who followed so-called 'beboppers' Charlie Parker and Dizzy Gillespie into uncharted territory.

One of the most stubbornly held canons of Revivalism was that there was no place in genuine New Orleans-style jazz for a saxophone of any denomination. This was later revealed as a myth, but died hard and is still upheld in some quarters. When Bruce appeared with the band at the Birmingham Town Hall and stepped forward to play his first solo on the dreaded instrument, the students from the nearby universities who thronged the hall unfurled a banner reading: 'GO HOME, DIRTY BOPPER'. In most matters, Bruce was highly sensitive, and from then until the end of his life he remained deeply suspicious of Birmingham and its jazz population.

It was some time earlier that we first discovered that we had imported serious eccentricity into our ranks. Onstage at the Picton Hall in Liverpool, Bruce's debut with us in a major venue, we were disturbed throughout the first half of the concert by an intermittent high-pitched squeak. At first we suspected the piano pedals, but our pianist Johnny Parker declared them innocent. In the interval, drummer George Hopkinson went on stage and checked the pedals of his bass drum and high-hat cymbals. They were in smooth working order. Halfway through the second half, with the mystery unsolved, I happened to turn round in time to see Bruce, mouth open like some great seabird, producing the dry creaking from somewhere in the depths of his oesophagus. Since it was his first gig with us, I decided to make no mention of it, especially as musically, he was performing at full, majestic throttle. After one of his high-flying solos, I went over to him and muttered 'Great, Bruce!' His answer was 'Nimrod!'

Over the eighteen years he was with me, in two stints between 1953 and 1988, I became quite well-versed in his idiosyncratic language and behaviour, stories of which have become the stuff of jazz legend and would alone fill a book of this size. His habit of uttering words and sentences in duplicate, of using outdated terminology in Billy Bunterish idiom – 'Some fun, I'd say!' 'This is the life for a chap!' (later abbreviated to 'Life for a chap, life for a chap!' and, eventually, just 'Chap, chap!') – his custom of calling all and sundry 'Dad' regardless of generation or gender and his strange, codified vocabulary that substituted 'Strawberry' for 'extraordinary' and enrolled 'Nimrod!' as an all-purpose exclamation – they have all seeped into the jazz language and ensured him some degree of immortality. As with many eccentrics, crazy happenings swarmed around him like flies round a donkey's eye.

Acker Bilk, with whom he worked in the sixties, remembers a day in Germany when he and other members of the band escorted Bruce to a shopping centre to help him buy a pair of shoes. Once assured that he was in the safe hands of an assistant who spoke English, they went off to do some shopping of their own. When they returned, they found the floor around Bruce strewn with discarded shoes and the salesman on the verge of suicide. It appeared that Bruce had tried on every shoe in the store, and not one would fit. Then a sharp-eyed member of the band spotted paper still in the toe of one shoe: 'Bruce, you haven't taken the paper out of the shoes!'

'Yeah!' cried Bruce to the bewildered salesman, 'Paper in the toe, Dad, paper in the toe!' When the musicians around him spontaneously broke into the familiar musical intro that, in tonic sol-fa, can be written SOH – SOH – soh – LA – LE – TE, the man must have concluded that his shop had been invaded by unfortunates on an outing from a secure institution.

In a band-room before one of our concerts, Bruce was talking about jazz to a fan who had found his way backstage. He crossed the room to ask me who had succeeded Peanuts Hucko as clarinettist in Louis Armstrong's All Stars. Neither he nor the fan could remember. Bruce said he thought the musician's name began with 's' and contained the letter 'i'. I couldn't help and he was still puzzling when we went on stage.

All through the first half of the concert, he kept coming across to me when someone else was soloing, muttering possibilities into my ear. 'Sykes . . . Spike . . . Styles . . . Shine . . .'. All drew a blank.

In the interval, he came over to say 'Think it might have started with a "P", started with a "P".' All through the second half, it was 'Price . . . Pike . . . Pyne . . . Pile . . .' in my ear, still with no result. Then, as we were preparing to leave after the show, he darted across the band-room to announce triumphantly, 'Got it, Dad, got it . . . it was Bob McCracken!'

Bruce was a lifelong teetotaller, one reason for which was his failure to find in the gamut of alcoholic refreshment anything that conformed to the demands of a sweet tooth of legendary proportion. I only saw him touch alcohol twice. When we were travelling in a coach on the Continent during a tour, he bought himself a bottle of Advocaat and almost drained it at one sitting, in the avowed belief that it was egg custard. When we reached our destination, he had to be walked round the block several times before he was fit to resume his career.

On another occasion, we were all relaxing in our hotel after a concert. Somebody ordered for him a Mackeson's Sweet Stout in the mistaken belief that the name would entice him to join in the fun. When it arrived he took one sip, crumpled his face in disgust and then, when he thought no one was looking, took a spoonful of brown sugar from a left-over coffee tray and tipped it into his glass.

For some reason that only a biochemist can explain, the drink instantly erupted, hissing, bubbling and steaming like a tropical geyser. It was a scene reminiscent of the dramatic moment in the old Jekyll and Hyde movie when Spencer Tracey, as Dr Jekyll, mixed the potion that was to transform him into Mr Hyde – except that Bruce, stopping short of metamorphosis, let out the squawk of a startled heron and then rounded on the donor of the sweet stout as if the poor man had done it on purpose.

Bruce died on 28 November 1993. His funeral in Milton Keynes was organised and conducted by his wife Sandra, and was a gloriously apt and joyful farewell. His love of music of every denomination, of theatre and literature and comedy, was celebrated along with his many idiosyncrasies. He was renowned for that sweet tooth, which prompted obsessive consumption of chocolate and cake. (We once played at a wedding and just in time prevented him from sampling the wedding cake before bride and bridegroom had even seen it.)

When at the start of his funeral the curtains went back to reveal his coffin, it was surmounted not with the customary pile of flowers, but by a large chocolate cake which Sandra had made for him. Into it, she had stuck a pennant bearing the initials BT. Bruce's ego manifested itself in mysterious ways. Coming across a drawerful of the pennants in some office or other, he had nicked a fistful of them. After his death, they were found by Sandra in a wardrobe. The initials stood for British Telecom.

I visited Bruce at their home in Newport Pagnell shortly before he died. As I left, Sandra handed me an envelope. It contained a letter that he wanted me to have. It was not addressed to anyone in particular, but it was clear when I read it that he wished it to be seen by his musical colleagues. Non-musicians need to know that the brief tremolo which instrumentalists employ at the end of a sustained note, to soften it or give it character, is called a 'terminal vibrato'. It is comforting to know that Bruce's love of humorous wordplay – silliness, perhaps – did not desert him even in his last days.

The letter read:

> Just to let you know that I am feeling pretty well, and in good spirits. I often wondered what it would be like to suffer from terminal vibrato, but it isn't bad really.
>
> Suddenly everyone is making me great stacks of cream pudding. I'm sure this can't be right, but I'm just letting it happen.
>
> Well, it is a bit of a nuisance about January. I thought I was going to do a few nice sessions round about that time, before calling it a day.
>
> Never mind, eh?
>
> Just want to say thanks for all the visits and kind greetings when I was laid up – it made me feel really

good. I loved 'Swinging Sounds for Sick Saxists', to which I have now added your earlier (Monday) programme and also the Steve Voce review [the reference is to broadcasts in tribute to him while he was in hospital, which he had put on tape]. Over generous, but still very nice to have.

I started out to write a longer letter than this, and to say how much I have valued all the friendships and good times I had while working with all you lot. But there is a danger of becoming treacly, so I'll stop here.

Bruce

Bruce Turner had been told by his Macmillan nurses that it was most unlikely that he would be able to get out and play in January. He died only a week or two after writing this letter, and it stands as an extraordinary act of bravery and selflessness.

*

To exemplify further the redeeming virtue of silliness, I summon some memories of my maternal grandfather.

Colonel Charles Adeane (like many of his generation he retained his military title after he retired from the army) was at various times a soldier, landowner, big-game hunter and, when I knew him, Lord Lieutenant of Cambridgeshire. In my eyes as a child, he was a terrifying tyrant prone to outbursts of impatience and appalling rudeness. In this respect, my grandmother was the perfect foil. In her young days, as Madeline Wyndham, she had been a noted beauty, as can be seen in a portrait of her with her two sisters painted by John Sargent and entitled *The Wyndham Sisters*. From the time we first knew her as small children, we regarded her as old, as children do. In that elongated old age, she was still remarkably handsome, with dignity enhanced by the sort of imposing and seemingly armour-plated bosom presented by her more famous contemporary, Queen Mary. She had grace and patience and we loved her. She entertained us in the evenings with card games – 'Snap' when we were small, the more complicated 'Bezique' when we were old enough. It is tempting to say that, in dealing with my grandfather's outbursts of rage and, on occasion, stubborn rudeness, her way with children stood her in good stead.

One evening when, as a teenager, I was staying at Babraham Hall, my grandparents' stately home in Cambridgeshire, two bachelor dons from Cambridge came to dinner. They had been invited by my grandmother, who took more seriously than her husband his duty, as Lord Lieutenant of the county, to maintain contact with nearby Cambridge University. As the meal progressed and the intellectual conversation rumbled on, I was aware of mounting restiveness at my grandfather's end of the table. When we stood up at the end, he said to me abruptly, 'Come on, Humphrey, we'll go and play billiards.'

It was a command to which there was no gainsaying, but as we went down to the billiard room in the basement, I thought it odd that he left his wife to entertain the two academics in the drawing room on her own. I felt even more uncomfortable when after an hour or so, Mr Fuller, the butler, came down to give the message from Mrs Adeane that the two gentlemen were leaving. We were in the middle of a game and, without turning from the table, he grunted, 'Mrs Adeane will say goodbye to them,' and played his shot. When we rejoined her after the two gentlemen had gone, she seemed quite unruffled. But I imagine that, in the privacy of the bedroom, he received at least a scolding.

I base that belief on a story that my father told, not without relish at its inherent humour.

The vicar of Babraham, whose church was in the grounds of Babraham Hall, was, as I remember, a blond, weedy little man of Uriah Heep-ish obsequiousness. In a moment of recklessness, he wrote to my grandfather complaining about the quality of the milk supplied by the Home Farm. My grandfather went straight to the bureau in the library and penned an outraged reply, berating the man for his impertinence. The letter ended with, 'I must ask you to get your milk elsewhere!' He showed it to my grandmother, who told him that he really could not post it – after all, they had to see the man in church every Sunday, not to mention discussing parish affairs with him at other times. Grudgingly, my grandfather tore up the letter and wrote another, only marginally less heated than the first. Once again, he ended, 'I must ask you to get your milk elsewhere!' And once again, my grandmother vetoed it.

The to-ing and fro-ing went on for a while until eventually my grandfather capitulated, writing a restrained letter expressing regret that the milk had been below standard and promising that the matter would be looked into and would never happen again. Testily, he signed it 'Yours sincerely, Charles Adeane' and handed it over. My grandmother read it and gave it back, saying, 'That's good – I'm sure it's best to do it that way.'

As my grandmother turned away, my grandfather hastily scrawled, 'I must ask you to get your milk elsewhere!' across the bottom, before sealing the letter in the envelope.

(There is a sequel to this story. The vicar concerned achieved widespread notoriety a few years later when the *News Of The World* reported that he had been found in bed with a Wall's Ice Cream man, thus giving an entirely new slant to the famous slogan 'Stop Me And Buy One.')

One further recollection of Charles Adeane underlines the power of silliness to redeem.

In stark contrast to the frightening image he presented to us children, Grandpapa, as we called him, had a party piece for which, at Christmas lunch, everyone clamoured, some indulgently, others enthusiastically, according to age and the number of times they had sat through the performance.

It told the story of a choppy cross-Channel voyage by a lady curiously named 'Mrs Yellowlily', an episode that required a few props and some preparation. He would first of all take a large Jaffa orange from the fruit bowl in the centre of the dining-room table and, with a sharp knife, prise out eyes and a gaping mouth. The latter he crammed with an assortment of raisins, sultanas, grapes and anything else that came to hand, finally furnishing it with teeth in the form of peeled almonds.

Draping a table napkin over a large wineglass, he put the effigy on top of it, and Mrs Yellowlily's journey began. As he intoned a running commentary, he gently manipulated the napkin so that the orange began to roll, gently at first, then grotesquely as the 'boat' moved into rougher seas. The climax came when the napkin was suddenly whisked away and the orange was squeezed into the glass, disgorging its assorted contents to the accompaniment of gleeful hawking and gagging sound effects from the Lord Lieutenant of Cambridgeshire.

Apart from the seasonal silliness described above, my grandfather had a gentle side that revealed itself to me in later years. He played the 'cello as a hobby, and I remember being encouraged by my mother more than once to go with her into the library at Babraham Hall to listen to him play. He played 'The Dying Swan' by Saint-Saëns with great feeling but he was not very expert, and there were moments when the thought occurred that a cow might have been a more appropriate subject. But as he sawed away, he adopted a dreamy, almost tragic expression, closing his eyes and flaring his nostrils with every groaning cadence. It was a sad look that, away from music, became more familiar in the years after my grandmother died and softens my memory of him.

It was many years after my father died that I discovered that he, too, had once played the 'cello. I could never imagine him handling a musical instrument, though given the choice, the voice and the talent, I think he would have made an impressive singer. Paul Robeson would have been his model. For a long time the choir in the Upper Chapel at Eton, which came from outside the school, boasted two formidable *basso profundi* known to boys and masters alike as Rumblebelly and Thunderguts. My father once canvassed their views on Robeson and was disappointed to learn that, notwithstanding the singer's cavernous and subterranean 'Ol' Man River', they judged him to be a bass/baritone rather than a true bass. The revelation didn't stop my father coming on like Paul Robeson in church, booming rather than singing the harmony parts of hymns or carols, while we glanced nervously around to see if anyone else was listening.

On one occasion, George Lyttelton was at an MCC dinner sitting with a friend and relative, Father Ted Talbot of the Mirfield Brotherhood of the Resurrection. One of them commented on the extraordinary volume of male bellowing around them that made normal conversation difficult. They decided to find out how loudly they could sing before anyone noticed. Thus, in a steady crescendo, the distinguished schoolmaster and the reverend cleric sang several verses of 'O God Our Help In Ages Past' before abandoning the fruitless exercise.

The surprising information about my father's flirtation with the 'cello came from a profile of him written for a university publication at the time he was up at Cambridge:

> When George Lyttelton practices the 'cello, all the cats in the district converge upon his rooms in the belief that one of their number is in distress.

I must say the sentence served to eradicate any vestigial sensitivity I might have retained about his views on my music, of which he once said, 'I understand it marginally less than I do Chinese.'

It occurs to me that, in discussing silliness, I may be blundering about in predominantly male territory. The historian Roger Fulford, who married my mother's sister Sibell and became a much-loved member of the family, believed that my mother was in fact funnier than my father in that her humour was less contrived.

Roger, small, pear-shaped and with the look of a quizzical mole, was himself delightfully droll company. It was he who jolted my father out of a deeply pessimistic mood at the outset of World War II. He responded to the wail of the first air-raid alarm to be heard in the Home Counties (a false alarm, as it turned out) with the pronouncement, in his fluting voice and with a twinkling eye, 'I regard it as the final fling of a desperate foe.' My father would still quote the knowingly absurd comment long after the war ended, six years later.

I saw much of Roger Fulford in those years through my close friendship with my cousin Anthony, of whom I wrote this in 1954:

> Anthony was really more of a brother-once-removed than a cousin to me, because our mothers are sisters and our fathers were brothers. We first met when I was eight and I disliked him so intensely that it was clear that we were either going to be deadly enemies or close friends. It turned out to be close friends. Our lives ran parallel – Sunningdale School, Eton, Wales and the Grenadiers – until he was killed on the Anzio beachhead in 1944.
>
> Anthony was more of a Lyttelton than I am. He was a sound, hard-working scholar (at Sunningdale he was always above me in class, which was humiliating because I was Lyttelton major and he was Lyttelton minor by a space of two months). He played cricket for Eton at Lord's and held strong but conservative tastes in music and the arts. If he had lived, I think he would have been the one to follow in my father's footsteps and maintain the Eton tradition on the staff at Eton.
>
> From my first book, *I Play As I Please* (McGibbon and Kee, 1954)

Looking back on it now, I would describe our relationship as something more akin to brotherly love. I was in bed at home in

Eton when, early one morning, my father came up to tell me that Anthony had been killed during what has since been revealed as the criminally futile invasion of Anzio in 1944. Delivering the news, he was too full of emotion to do more than blurt out the information in a choked voice before giving me a rough, consolatory shake of the shoulder and hurrying from the room.

I had not long been back from Italy on sick leave after my own dehumanising experiences of death on the beachhead at Salerno. In the dark moments of the night, I'm sometimes disturbed by the absence of any great surge of grief in my recollection of that early morning, but rather a numb feeling of, 'Well, that's that.'

Not much of an epitaph for someone who was a brother in all respects other than actual joint parenthood. But war is destructive in ways that reach far beyond the obvious. As things turned out, our lives would probably have veered off in quite different directions after the war. But the fact is that he played the brotherly role, with all its companionship and petty vicissitudes, throughout the years when it was most important – and the most fun to remember.

As Roger Fulford perceived, style of humour was one of the areas in which my father and mother differed from (I prefer to say complemented) each other. These excerpts, from communications that I had from each of them at various times, will perhaps highlight the contrasting styles.

While he was visiting an old friend, the author Percy Lubbock, at his villa near Via Reggio in Italy, my father sent me a postcard in which he wrote:

> I breakfast in bed every morning, getting up just in time for a three-course lunch. The afternoon, however, is less strenuous. The food is delicious and the waistline prospers. But have we not all eternity to bant in?

NOTES

1. The now obsolete word 'bant', meaning in late Victorian times to diet, derived from the name of William Banting, who in

1863 wrote the first book on low-carbohydrate diet 'as a service to his fellow man' (a service which to some observers today might put him in roughly the same category as the fictional Doctor Frankenstein!)

2. It has come as no surprise to me to learn, lately, that my father, who could summon from his capacious memory a literary quotation to match every possible occasion, borrowed the final rhetorical sentence almost verbatim from the nineteenth-century essayist Thomas Carlyle, who used it in response to his wife's insistence that he should rest.

It was in somewhat similar circumstances that my mother wrote to me in January 1974 from Dorset, where she had spent a family Christmas at the home of my elder sister Diana and her husband, Alexander Viscount Hood. In response in each case to a lifestyle more lavish than their own, my father revealed epicurean leanings while my mother's were emphatically stoic. She wrote:

> We started dinner one night with caviar – a tiny little pot for seven people. I made a mental note of the cost and rushed upstairs and sent £5 to Help The Aged as a peace offering! Caviar means nothing to me – kipper paste is more in my line!

My mother kept a diary during a short period of her life. She was the eldest of six children. It was the strict custom of the day that, as such, she should remain at home when the other fledglings had flown, to be a help to her mother and a companion to her father. Even in the emergency of world war, this rule applied; so when my mother, already in her mid-twenties, expressed a wish to join the VAD (Voluntary Aid Detachments) as many of her contemporaries were doing, the notion was sternly vetoed by my grandfather. After much persuasion, he grudgingly agreed that she could go with friends on a nursing course in East Anglia. While there, she wrote to him to say that she would not be his daughter if she did not enlist to do her bit.

The implied flattery did the trick and in July 1916, she went to France. She was already engaged to my father (they eventually married in 1919) and she was accompanied by his sister Rachel Lyttelton and cousin Hermione (her friends on the course). It was at the time of the prolonged Battle of the Somme and she was posted immediately to a hospital outside Rouen, not far behind the front-line trenches, her friends either with her or in hospitals nearby.

Pamela Adeane circa 1918.

During her time in France she kept the diary. As might be expected of someone brought up in an aristocratic home where reticence and self-control were instilled, her account was muted of the horrors which she must have witnessed as convoys of wounded and dying soldiers, many still in their teens, were brought in. At one point she wrote of, 'the sadness and horror of seeing so much suffering and death', adding characteristically, 'I can remember it all very distinctly, but think it best not to write down all the details.' The following excerpts, however, paint a picture all the more sombre for the juxtaposition of tragedy and the stuff of holiday postcards home. She had arrived in France in mid-July, and by 2 August was writing this:

I had my off-duty time this afternoon and sat and wrote letters in the orchard near our quarters. Ogilvie, a young Australian of eighteen years, who reminds me of a St Bernard puppy or a young colt with large, loose-jointed limbs, is desperately ill in the ward. He has a wound in the back which is infected with gas gangrene and he is dying of septic poisoning. This evening I stood by him all the time I was on duty so as to do the little that could be done to make him more comfortable. He was very restless but very patient and kept saying that he would be better in the morning, but I do not think he will live till morning. It is very sad and painful, and the thought of these young Australians and Canadians dying so far from their homes is very affecting.

3 August. Went on duty and found that Ogilvie had died in the night.

The manner in which this second entry continues, here abridged, reveals the extraordinary mental adjustment that seems to click in almost automatically in the grotesque circumstances of war:

I had my off-duty time in the afternoon and R. had an off-day, so we went down to Rouen and met H. in the cathedral. It is a heavenly cool and peaceful place to sit in. The heat in the streets and trams is appalling and they are both very crowded. I hate the feeling of being jammed up among so many hot people. We stayed about three-quarters of an hour and then went with H. who wanted to cash a cheque at Cox's and do some shopping.

My mother was in France for eleven months before becoming ill herself. The diary ends with her return to England, and this epilogue:

A diary is a very egotistical thing, and it is rather difficult not to make it sound as though one was the only person who had done anything! The thing to remember is that there are thousands of VADs and that I served less long and with less powers of endurance than most of them!

It appears that her maternal grandmother, also called Madeline, read the diary some time later. Using the generic nickname given to generations of Wyndham and Adeane grandmothers she added, in heavy pencil, this forceful postscript:

> Gan-gan does not agree. She knows that you worked hard and through many months after your bodily strength had quite broken down, simply on your spirit, determination and resolution . . . And therefore it was heroic. M Wyndham, August 1918

My own experience of the horrors of front-line warfare was far shorter, a mere five weeks in 1943 before a cocktail of illnesses brought it to an end. The actual landing on the Salerno beachhead was a protracted and brutal episode. In written and spoken reminiscences, I have focussed on what some would call the frivolous side, which is nowadays brought back to me frequently by people whose names and faces I don't recognise saying such things as, 'I remember you playing your trumpet at Salerno, serenading us at night with a jazzed-up version of 'The Last Post.' This was less irreverent than it sounds nowadays, since the functional, as opposed to ceremonial, purpose of that sombre bugle-call was simply to convey to troops in the field the order 'Lights Out!'

Nevertheless it contrasts shockingly with a stronger memory I have from that same period. A sergeant with whom I worked as a signals officer was brought back into the battalion headquarters to die. The once strong, handsome, confident man was trying to raise his shattered body from the stretcher, crying pitifully, 'Mummy, Mummy!' I am no psychiatrist, but putting that ever-present but rarely summoned recollection alongside my mother's more expansive memories does focus on the mind's capacity to divide itself, in moments of extreme and abnormal horror, into two quite separate compartments, one for things of which 'it is best not to write down all the details', the other for trips to the shops or the beachhead trumpeting.

PS: A decade or more after the end of World War I, my mother and father took me and my older sister Diana on a short holiday to Bruges in Belgium from where we visited such places as the notorious Hill 60 and the site of the vast long-distance cannon nicknamed Big Bertha. I still have a small replica of a field-gun, green with age and verdigris, to remind me of what fun it all was. I imagine that, so far as we children were concerned, the purpose of the visit was educational. For my mother, of course, it was a different thing. I remember us, on one occasion, standing on high ground overlooking a war cemetery, a huge field filled with row upon row of small white crosses perfectly aligned like a battalion on parade. In the silence, I glanced at my mother. Tears were pouring down her face.

*

Bringing Roger Fulford into the hotchpotch leads me to observe that the dividing line between silliness and eccentricity is narrow but clearly defined. In 1933, he wrote a glorious book entitled *The Wicked Uncles*, subtitled *The Father Of Queen Victoria And His Brothers*. Of the five uncles, the most sympathetic – better, perhaps, to say the least unattractive – was Adolphus Frederick, Duke of Cambridge, whom the author describes as:

> a grave disappointment to those sparkling letter-writers, those acid diarists, those resourceful chatterers and the Whig historians who are, in their respective spheres, responsible for the history of England. There could be no room in their pages or their talk for a prince who was dutiful, sober, moral and honoured his father and mother.

Adolphus owes his place in this book of mine to an eccentricity which appears to have spiralled out of control towards the end of his life:

> His finest and most eccentric efforts were reserved for church. He became very deaf and always sat right in the front of the church, where he was seen by the whole congregation. This might not have been so serious if he had not made a practice of being heard all over the church as well, in a running commentary on the service. It was a common occurrence to hear in reply to the clergyman's 'Let us pray,' an agreeable 'By all means' from the Duke, or, in answer to a prayer for rain, 'Amen, but you won't get it till the wind changes,', or, in answer to the sentence, 'For we brought nothing into the world, neither may we carry anything out,' the reply, 'True, true – too many calls upon us for that.'

Roger Fulford's account concludes:

> A clergyman, who was in the congregation, taking no part in the service, has given a graphic description of the Duke in prayer: 'I had not caught what psalm the clerk had given out and turning to look on my neighbour's page, fidgety restless HRH turns round and bawls loud enough to drown the organ, "It begins at the third verse, the third verse." All eyes turned on Royalty speaking to inferior clergy. Royalty went on singing like a bull.

The Wicked Uncles by Roger Fulford (G P Putnam's Sons, New York, 1933)

The Lyttelton family tree has its fair crop of eccentrics. I believed until quite recently that I was named after the Humphrey Lyttelton who was hanged in the aftermath of the Gunpowder Plot for harbouring the conspirators, and that the name was banned by the family from that day onwards until my father chose it as an act of defiance. It appears that this is fantasy. A woman attending one of my gigs in Worcestershire left for me a photograph that she thought might interest me. It was of a plaque in her nearby village church in memory of a Humphrey Lyttelton who died a natural death some twenty years after the Plot.

Not long after that revelation, word reached me that yet another Humphrey Lyttelton was buried in a tomb in a church at King's Norton, near Birmingham, during the same century. As my long-running Radio 2 programme, *The Best of Jazz*, has for the last decade been recorded in Birmingham, I took time off to see for myself. And there it was, a large marble sarcophagus bearing the name Humphrey Lyttelton, on the lid of which is a faded depiction of a rather dashing-looking man with what used to be known as a Van Dyke beard lying alongside his wife who, it was believed, shared the tomb with him. The belief was misguided. The discovery of another tomb bearing his name in a church in nearby Pershore revealed that, having had himself depicted alongside his wife in King's Norton, he had high-tailed it to Pershore, as fit as a fiddle, to marry again and live for another twenty-odd years.

So far as I know, history does not record whether he was an accomplished con man or an early Lyttelton eccentric. Personally, I wish history would keep its mouth shut. The original Gunpowder Plot theory at least offered some anecdotal compensation for having been christened Humphrey.

It's a consoling fact that these days, anyone named Humphrey will soon become known as 'Humph'. When polite people of brief acquaintance ask, 'Do you mind if I call you Humph?' I answer eagerly, 'Oh, please do!' I didn't acquire the abbreviation in childhood. Most of my close relatives have preferred Hump, which I find less – well, comfy, though it does supply a fathomless source of merriment whenever the warning 'Humps Ahead' is encountered on the roadside.

When I began to draw cartoons for the *Daily Mail* in the late forties, I signed them 'humph' with a small 'h'. So if there are any disadvantages derived from the pen-name – such as finding

myself turning round enquiringly when large dogs bark 'Humph! Humph!' in the street – I have perhaps only myself to blame.

I have suggested that I am not very keen on the name Humphrey. It seems sort of stuffy and, were there such an adjective, upholstery, like the padding on some rather musty old boarding-house sofa. But it seems to be extraordinarily popular as a name for animals. One has only to think of Humphrey, the famous Downing Street cat, recently deceased but no doubt already enshrined in history.

Fewer people are likely to know of a camel in Edinburgh Zoo who, for the run of a promotional campaign during the Zoo's brief sponsorship of the Edinburgh International Jazz Festival, was wittily renamed Humprey. I had my photograph taken with him, but I can't say that we struck up a close relationship. Like camels of any age, he looked moth-eaten and as if bits were quietly dropping off him. Nevertheless I was pleased for him when, re-visiting the Zoo the following year, I saw that his original name, Ptolemy II, had been restored, along with his dignity.

Then there was Guide Dog Humphrey, a magnificent Alsatian whose photograph hangs in my loo. Again it was a publicity promotion that brought us together. We were photographed in one-sided conversation in the centre of a small but busy roundabout on the outskirts of Walsall – of all places to be seen lying belly down on the grass talking to a dog!

I have postponed to the end the ill-fated budgerigar called Humphrey who was adopted in my honour as a mascot by the crew of a Royal Navy submarine. One day, when the hatches were battened down and the vessel was submerged, Humphrey managed to escape from his cage. In a tragically brief moment of freedom, he flew straight into the ventilator fan. I imagine that the captain of the vessel was still picking feathers out of his nostrils when he wrote to me a few days later to break the sad news.

Some time in 2004, I received a postcard from a musical associate saying that, on holiday in Egypt, he and his partner were gazing at a statue that had been defaced with graffiti when she spotted, high up, the name and date 'A Lyttelton 1839'. Coincidence, perhaps, but it set my mind trawling through possible offenders among my forebears. It's unlikely to have been Great Uncle Alfred Lyttelton, who captained England at cricket and was Colonial Secretary in his spare time. Very little information was ever handed down to me about Great Uncle Arthur other than that he became Bishop of Southampton, so I must put him down as unpromising. My money would be on Great Uncle Albert, who provided much anecdotal fodder in his time.

I have often told the story of one of Albert Victor Lyttelton's most famous exploits, but have lately discovered that I have tweaked it out of recognition. It was my father who told it to me in the first place, and fortunately his account appears in one of the letters he wrote to Rupert Hart-Davis. It's better that he should tell it himself:

> Some day you might like to hear of my Uncle Albert. He was *not* humdrum. He was a missionary. His face, his saintliness and, to a certain extent, his clothes and his diet were those of John the Baptist. He was insatiably curious. When moving staircases came in, he tried to stop one by holding on to one of the stationary knobs at the side. A moment later he picked himself up from the floor, quite

satisfied by the proof that he could *not* stop it. Then he tried (about sixty-odd) to go *up* the stairs that were coming *down*, and after a minute or so on what must have been exactly like a treadmill, found out that that wouldn't do either.

From *The Lyttelton–Hart-Davis Letters* (John Murray)

I have no source of verification for the following story, nor do I know where it came from. But it sounds in character.

When, as a missionary, Albert Lyttelton was posted to South Africa, he had occasion to make a long train journey from Johannesburg to Durban. He was waiting outside his house for the cab that had been summoned to take him to the station, which was overdue. Anxious about the time, he pulled his fob watch by its chain out of his waistcoat pocket. Insecurely attached, the watch flew off the chain and smashed on to the pavement. Without hesitation, he went back indoors and took an ornate ormolu clock off the mantelpiece. Thenceforward, his long journey was uneventful as he rattled across the South African *veld* holding the large clock carefully upright on his lap with its pendulum ticking noisily.

Despite the somewhat fanatical John the Baptist appearance, Albert was undoubtedly a sweet man, as this brief account of another train journey suggests.

During a tiring journey in England, Albert went into an empty waiting room to rest. Finding the narrow, slatted seating round the walls unconducive to relaxation, he lay down on the floor. A young couple entered the waiting room, chattering and laughing until their eyes fell on the large, bearded and recumbent cleric and they were struck dumb. Without moving, Albert opened one eye and reassured them in a gentle voice, 'Not drunk. Just tired.'

The reader will have gathered that I'm riddled with doubt about some of these stories handed down to me. Did I really have a great-aunt on my mother's side, who became so small in her old age that when she sat at the dinner table, food reached her mouth solely by the force of gravity? (I detect my father's imprint on that one.) Once again, I turn for guidance to the Chairman:

> It matters not if stories of our quirks and foibles pass, through repetition and embroidery, from fact into fiction. They are, after all, the stuff of immortality.
>
> Chairman Humph, in Johnsonian mode

I certainly remember with affection my father's sister, Maud Wyndham (Wyndhams appear on both sides of my family, just to be confusing). She was so vague that her utterances, wandering through a maze of innumerable cul-de-sacs, rarely managed to reach a full stop. But I have to take on trust the story that staying with relatives in the country, she was asked by a solicitous host at breakfast if she had been disturbed at dawn by the singing of the birds. She answered, 'Oh, but not singing – yellin'!'

(Like many of her generation, Aunt Maud affected elements of what is imprecisely known as a 'cockney accent', such as dropping the terminal 'g' in 'yelling'. She would regularly use 'ain't' for 'aren't' in an otherwise lofty, aristocratic voice. I have already noted the ubiquitous aberrations 'lorst' and 'gorn', which I inherited but appear to have shed without trying. I imagine they came from the same source. I learnt recently from the radio that no less a person than Queen Victoria spoke her English with this hybrid pronunciation, referring to soldiers as 'sodgers'). Aunt Maud wafts in and out of my memory like a welcome and benign ghost. I was better acquainted with my father's youngest brother, Richard Lyttelton, whose eccentricity was on a grander scale.

It was thrown into high relief by the fact that Richard was a businessman who eventually reached the position of President of the Iron and Steel Federation. Despite this, he appeared to live in the belief that bankruptcy was just around the corner. His city attire, though conventional in that it involved the customary black suit with pinstriped trousers, was so old that the trousers had worn threadbare in several places and had been patched with rectangles of plain black material. He clearly didn't believe that this was in any way extraordinary. My father, who assisted Richard with references and anecdotes whenever he had to speak on a formal occasion, reported that his brother's dinner suit was so old that it had turned green.

Richard was my godfather. On visits to Eton, he would quite often remember the fact, pressing a ten-shilling note into my hand when he left to go home. There were occasions when, in his vagueness, he pressed it mistakenly into Anthony's hand, unwittingly stoking the cousinly rivalry between us.

It was hard for him to forget my Confirmation, and he came down to Eton for the service. Afterwards, he gave me a mono-grammed half-hunter gold watch from Mappin & Webb, which I still have. I have no doubt that he handed it over with some sound godfatherly advice, but it would have been delivered in such a hesitant and meandering fashion that I would not have taken it in. I do, however, remember his concern that I should tell him if in any way it didn't perform properly, ending with the gloriously orotund phrase, 'If not, I shall have words with Mappin not wholly unaccompanied by Webb.' The watch has worked perfectly for 67 years and is ticking away in a rather self-satisfied way on my desk as I write.

Richard Lyttelton played a pivotal role in my life, since it was through him that in the early forties, I and my cousin Anthony came to spend eighteen months in the Guest Keen Baldwin steelworks in South Wales.

He once came to see us at Port Talbot, to see how we were getting on. We were in a manager's office when someone came in to say, 'Your uncle's here.' We went out, to find him standing amidst the massive entrails of the coke oven plant, looking, with his formal black overcoat and hard-brimmed Homburg hat, as if arriving at a board meeting. It was typical of his diffidence that he hadn't come straight into the office himself, preferring to teeter around amid the rubble in Monsieur Hulot fashion. As we approached, he greeted us with, 'Oh . . . yes . . . well, here we are.' Then after a short, characteristic laugh – a single falsetto 'Ha!' – he looked up at the overhead workings and said 'Pipes.' The vagueness was clearly his way of bridging an awkward gap when the conventional greeting 'Hello' eluded him.

My mother shared with her sister, Sibell Fulford, the belief that the vagueness which Richard Lyttelton and his sister Maud displayed (and indeed the diffidence shown by the whole of that generation of the family), stemmed from the domineering character of my paternal grandmother. Try as I may, I can't ever remember Granny on the move. She's always sitting in a chair, a formidable figure, not unlike Queen Victoria in stature and appearance, with both hands before her firmly pressing on the handle of a walking stick in an attitude of authority. A story has been handed down of how, as a child, my father made her a crudely stitched stuffed tiger as a Christmas present, as children then and sometimes now are encouraged to do, only to have it flung contemptuously across the room with the words, 'Don't ever give me anything as horrible as that again.' And I remember both my mother and Sibell recalling separately visiting the family's London home in their courting days, to find their respective husbands-to-be, both men in their thirties, while not actually standing in the corner, at least being given a dressing-down like naughty schoolboys.

There is evidence that Granny Cobham (somewhere along the line the eldest Lyttelton sons acquired the title of Viscount Cobham) concealed a vein of eccentricity beneath the stern exterior. When an old lady, she surprised visiting grandchildren with the announcement, uttered slowly and with emphasis, 'Harrods . . . never stop sending me . . . riding breeches.'

Richard Lyttelton and his wife Judith lived in Highgate. At one stage they took a holiday cottage in Epping Forest, to which my cousin and I were often invited to help with DIY operations that principally involved whitewashing the walls. Family gatherings there were frequent.

On one occasion, at an informal lunch, Uncle Richard stood behind my Aunt Sibell's chair, rather inexpertly opening a quart bottle of cider. Having presumably been shaken up on its way to the table, the bottle erupted with a hiss, the froth drenching my aunt. She let out a shriek of surprise which would, in a normal social situation, have prompted profuse apology and solicitous, if ineffective, mopping of her person with a pocket-handkerchief. From Uncle Richard came the familiar 'Ha!' and the comment, 'Ah . . . yes, well . . . cottage noises!'

In Highgate Grove, Richard was a well-known and extremely popular figure, often to be seen, before his eventual retirement, setting off for his office in the City on his bicycle. As he whizzed down Parliament Hill, peddling energetically, passers-by would surely have spotted darting flashes of pink leg between trouser and shoe. In the days of strict clothes rationing during and after World War II, he conserved his coupons by giving up socks. The financial advantages of this decision did not escape him and though austerity eventually ended, he never wore them again.

I have not inherited the family pessimism in financial matters. When I visited Uncle Richard once in the City, I took a taxi from Swiss Cottage, where we then lived, without giving the matter a thought, though I was at the time an impecunious art student. Unwisely, I confessed the extravagance to Richard, whose response was, 'Oh, well, yes, we can't have that . . . money's money . . .' then the familiar falsetto 'Ha!' The thought flashed through my mind that he was going to offer me a free ride home in a company limousine but, as expectations go, it wasn't very robust. When our meeting was over, he came down with me to the street and walked me to the bus stop, hovering until I was safely on board. I waited until we were round a bend and out of sight before I hopped off and hailed a taxi.

When it comes to answering the question 'Fact or fiction?' in such recollections, I'm quite content to remain in a perpetual quandary over the enviable cast of dotty relatives owned or invented by the American humorous writer and cartoonist James Thurber. I warm especially to his cousin several times removed (but luckily not too far), Gracie Shoaf, of whom he wrote in these terms:

> She was confident that burglars had been getting into her house every night for forty years. The fact that she never missed anything was to her no proof to the contrary. She always claimed that she had scared them off before they could take anything, by throwing shoes down the hallway. When she went to bed, she piled, where she could get at them handily, all the shoes there were about her house. Five minutes after she had turned off the light she would sit up in bed and say, 'Hark!' Her husband, who had learned to ignore the whole situation as long ago as 1903, would either be sound asleep or pretend to be sound asleep. In either case he would not respond to her tugging and pulling, so that presently she would arise, tiptoe to the door, open it slightly and heave a shoe down the hall in one direction, and its mate down the hall in the other direction. Some nights she threw them all, some nights only a couple of pairs.

> *Vintage Thurber* James Thurber

Thurber came nearer to home with this reminiscence:

> My mother thought – or rather, knew – that it was dangerous to drive an automobile without gasoline; it fried the valves or something. 'Now, don't you dare drive all over town without gasoline!' she would say to us when we started off.

Mothers tend, more often than fathers, to invite affectionate mockery. Louis Armstrong recalled, in his first autobiography *Satchmo* (Peter Davis Ltd, 1955) that if, as a child, he did something foolish, his mother would persistently liken him to Fatty O'Butler, meaning the rotund Hollywood comedian, Fatty Arbuckle.

My own mother had problems with names on the radio. It's not unusual. When it comes to accurate identification, radio is a tricky medium, relying solely on the ear, without back-up from the eye. If ever I mention in my jazz programme the New Orleans-born, and subsequently Ellingtonian clarinettist Barney Bigard, I expect to receive queries from one or more listeners who assume that his first name is Barnaby. And until she came more closely into focus as my supremo on BBC Radio, I never quite got to grips with the name of Jenny Abramsky. Was the surname O'Bramsky or just plain Bramsky? In the latter option the forename Jennia or Gennia seemed improbable. I'm sure she has not got where she is today without being made aware of this confusion.

With my mother, there were two main stumbling blocks. One was the erstwhile newsreader, Alvar Liddell (with the accent on the last syllable). Thinking that he was Mr Bollidel, she felt at that time that it was rather vulgar for a BBC newsreader to be known as Al. Worse was the leader of the Scottish Symphony Orchestra in days gone by who was regularly announced as J. Mouland Begby. She once said to me, 'I can understand Jane Wool, though it's not a common name. But who is Begby?'

It is indeed a mistake that conjures up a Thurberesque image of a manic woman, manifestly at war with her male conductor, sawing away furiously at the fiddle with a large, shapeless dog called Begby at her elbow.

Having strayed into the realms of comic writing, I must pay homage to two other heroes. The late Patrick Campbell's articles, written for a variety of publications, stand as a reproach to that *Daily Mail* deputy editor who scolded me, misquoting along the way. To devote, as Campbell gloriously did, a whole article to a sneeze is surely piling Ossa on Pelion and throwing in Olympus for good measure. This extract from an essay headed 'The Stallion Sneeze' describes the onset of what turned out to be a cataclysmic explosion when, working at his desk and eating an *ad hoc* breakfast at the same time, he had just popped a large tomato, peppered and salted, into his mouth.

> First this giant force got to work upon my jaws and mouth, pressing out and hardening the delicate machinery until with the teeth bared and the upper lip drawn back I must have looked like Silver, the mad stallion, about to do something unpleasant. At the same time this frightful pressure squeezed my eyes shut and then shoved them along the Eustacian tubes into my ears, where they flung themselves against the drums, trying to get out. This displacement of the eyes led almost immediately to a change in the shape of the top of my head. It began to rise into a point, with the subsidiary effect of drawing me right up into the top left-hand corner of my high-backed chair, so that it seemed that I retained a grip upon the floor only with a single toe. For some time I held this pose, levitating, teeth bared, lips curled, nostrils flaring, eyes gone, ears bursting and nails dug deep into the upholstery. Then everything blew up . . .

Several paragraphs later, he describes the aftermath:

> The extremely high muzzle velocity of the breakfast had enabled it to reach and to penetrate every corner and crevice of the room. It had got to the bookshelf and to the Modigliani reproduction above it. It was on the door, the ceiling and all four walls. It was in the typewriter. It had even struck a portrait of me painted by an aunt of mine in 1954, where it had obliterated one eye. The other stared back at me in outrage.

Prelude to a sneeze.

Nancy Banks-Smith – now, alas, only a sporadic television reviewer in the *Guardian* newspaper – must stand as one of the nation's great comic writers. I search the bookstalls in vain for an anthology of her articles. If it exists and I come across it, I hope and expect that it would contain these comments on a TV programme called *Vegetable Plots*. The programme was about an autumn fayre in Ponders End.

> The autumn show is a demonstration of vegetable love, vaster than empires. Onions that look as if the Kremlin had come to Ponders End and pupped. A pumpkin that took two men to carry it. 'Stay there!' said Tony. 'Don't move!' said Tommy, as if it might suddenly rise on its vast haunches like a Sumo wrestler and attack . . . Bill's cabbages seemed on the point of explosion. He trundled them in on a wheelbarrow, which squealed in protest. Like Grandfather's clock they were too big for the bench, so he stood them on the floor. They peered out from beneath the bench with bulging, deep green eyes fringed with vast lashes.

Nancy Banks-Smith in a television review in the *Guardian*

People often speak of an 'English sense of humour', and it's no more accurate than most such generalisations. It's not a matter of nationality. The distinction is between lateral and literal thinking. I recall an edition of the long-running TV show *Have I Got News For You* that brought together two great contemporary British fantasists, Paul Merton and Ross Noble. Their interplay on the programme was a masterclass in lateral thinking, the process of leading a mundane thought or statement off on a trail of fantasy that takes it far from its literal source.

This baffles those of a literal frame of mind, who can't follow the trail. They in turn will be thought by lateral-thinkers to resemble the horrid little boy at a children's party who shouts, 'It's not him talking – it's you!' at the ventriloquist who is doing his best to create a fantasy. I recently heard someone on the radio – and I can't attribute it since it came and went too quickly for me to jot it down – quoting some high-ranking German personage as saying, 'The German nation has many shortcomings but I'm glad to say a sense of humour is not one of them!'

I have an account, given to me by the great comedian Les Dawson, of a meeting that he and a colleague once had with a female television producer. Read this story in any accent you choose. Let's just say that the producer came from a culture in which literal thinking predominates. She was interested in transferring some of the Les Dawson shows for Yorkshire Television on to her country's TV screens. 'Abortive' is the word that immediately springs to mind, but the discussion went ahead. As they read to her examples of sketches from some chosen scripts, the eagerness slipped slowly but inexorably from her face, to be replaced by blank incomprehension.

When it seemed that, in Arthur Daley's words, a 'nice little earner' was going down the plughole, Les said in desperation that his shows included what they called 'shorties' – wordless visual cartoons that lasted no more than thirty seconds or so. Perking up a little at the idea, she asked for an example. He then described one in which he is first seen as a road sweeper at the far end of a residential street. Without a word being spoken, he advances slowly towards the camera, pushing his brush before him. When he reaches the foreground of the shot, he lifts the corner of the kerb, carpet-fashion, shoves the accumulated rubbish under it, replaces it and shuffles on round the corner. Les and his colleague looked at her expectantly as she pondered on what she had seen. Then she shook her head sadly and said with a shrug, 'The trouble is, at home we do not have these pavements that lift up.'

My own fondness for humour that leans towards the surrealistic was honed in my teenage years by regular visits to the variety theatre, usually with other siblings or cousins, booked and presided over by my Aunt Maud who, as I have described earlier, was herself surrealism personified.

Nothing in more modern theatre has excited me more than those now extinct shows, with the widely varied acts logged by numbers on an illuminated sign at the side of the stage. 'Yippee! Eight more to go! . . . Oh dear, only two left!' Schoolboy emotions ebbed and flowed. I may be amalgamating several visits into one experience when I recall having seen Max Miller, Gracie Fields and the Mills Brothers in one show. Small details alone remain: of the Mills Brothers singing 'Paper Doll' with father Harry 'boom-boom-booming' in imitation of a double bass; of Gracie, raucous and down-to-earth until the headscarf was donned to herald the sentimental bits; of Max Miller's wicked eyes glinting and darting in the spotlight, an unnaturally vivid blue like modern laser headlights.

One substantial memory that has stayed with me over the years is of a favourite and now largely forgotten comedian, Sidney Howard. Stout and pear-shaped, he walked with the careful gait and out-turned hands of someone gingerly crossing a stream on a plank, and spoke with the pomposity and frayed gentility of a rather seedy butler. Relating this story in my own words, I'll try to convey something of his ponderous delivery.

The Queen of some Ruritanian country summoned all the magicians and conjurors in the realm to perform for her, offering a lavish prize for the one whom she adjudged the best. Things were not going well until it came to a performer who, to launch his act, requested her to unclasp and hand to him the priceless ruby pendant, suspended by a slim gold chain, that adorned her capacious bosom. He took a mortar and pestle and, while she watched in some dismay, placed the precious jewel in it and ground it to dust. The assembled company gasped as he opened a casement window and scattered the dust to the four winds. After a dramatic pause, he clapped his hands three times and a white dove, appearing as if from nowhere, flew into the room bearing in its beak the ruby, suspended on its gold chain and restored to its pristine beauty. Overcome with relief and admiration, the Queen summoned him to stand before her. In a gracious speech, she pronounced him the winner of the contest. And then, as drums rolled, she dipped her hand into her corsage and presented him with a sofa and three easy chairs.

Without making exaggerated claims, it should be noted that this tale, told at some time in the mid-thirties, pre-dated by at least two decades the arrival of the so-called 'shaggy dog' story.

A recollection has occurred . . .

I must confess that I'm not very fond of the word 'bullshit'.

The Revd Donald Soper, chatting in a TV green room as we waited our call on a Terry Wogan radio show in the seventies

As an orator for many years on London's Speakers' Corner near Marble Arch, the late Donald Soper must have been exposed to the whole gamut of rude language. I respected his view on that and, indeed, on pretty well everything else. But a distinction has to be drawn between the origins of so-called 'rude words' and their subsequent usage, much of it spread over such a large area as to have become sanitised.

> You can rarely check in at a surgery, hotel or airport reception without seeing someone behind the desk staring in blank incomprehension at a screen, jabbing frantically at a keyboard and repeating over and over again the words 'Oh, shit!'

Chairman Humph, in hi-tech mode

If any readers experience an involuntary intake of breath at my use of that word, I must ask them to say what it means in that context. The answer is, nothing, it's just a syllable that people find effective for letting off steam. In fact, the more vehemently you say it, the more appropriately onomatopoeic it sounds. In this matter, I am on the side of freedom of speech. I could have used euphemism, quoting the exasperated receptionists as saying, 'Oh, crumbs!' or, more daringly, 'Oh, tiddle!' But that would be both inaccurate and absurd.

There are, indeed, situations in which it seems sensible to use the word in its original meaning. You wouldn't expect me to say other than that humour is at the top of my list. It was from Les Dawson that I heard a brief gag that defies euphemism or circumlocution.

In the early sixties, BBC radio ran a series of variety shows called *Home and Away*. Two teams of artists and musicians were assembled, the lucky ones touring British army barracks for four nights in Germany, the losers appearing for one night at the Nuffield Centre in London. I was one of the lucky ones. The show in which I went to Germany included the Ronnie Aldrich Trio as house band, impressionist Peter Goodright as the compère, Les Dawson as the young, up-and-coming comic, Elkie Brooks as the young, up-and-coming singer and myself as the not-so-young, been-around-for-yonks jazz instrumentalist.

Each day, we travelled about two hundred miles from one army station to another. Peter Goodright and Les Dawson sat together on the coach, and at the start of each trip, they asked us to give them a topic. They would then ad-lib a non-stop stream of gags on the topic of the day until we reached our destination, honing their skills as stand-up comedians are wont to do. In a marathon on the subject of 'Holidays', Les came up with what I deem to be the perfect joke – short, concise and with a false ending and a punchline that lives up to the description:

> The staff of a sewage farm in the North of England went on a day's outing to Blackpool. One of their number was overcome by the fresh air and fainted. [Pause here to allow tittering] . . . It took seven buckets of shit to bring him round!

If you recount that gag to your friends, you are free to insert a euphemism – fertiliser, perhaps, or even Number Twos, you quaint old thing – if you wish. But don't blame me if it collapses like an under-baked soufflé.

Another reason for the forthright use of an impolite word occurred to me not long ago. It appeared on the wall of my local doctors' surgery, a handwritten poster that drew attention to an important, perhaps life-saving statistic. It was headed: 'SHIT!' Underneath, it went on to say, 'Did you know that one gram of poo contains one thousand varieties of bacteria?'

I may not have the statistic right, but the message is clear. Note that the writer, having written the startling headline with bravado, suffered a sudden spasm of guilt and retreated into childish euphemism.

Here, with unaccustomed athleticism, I will do a somersault and argue that euphemism too, has its place in humour, and the more absurd the better.

No one would describe my father as a ghoul, but he did have a fascination for murder trials, whether factual or fictional. He always read through the crime reports in his local paper. After his death, a cutting was found, brown and faded, in his desk. (There's no doubt he kept it for its absurdity, rather than its gruesome content.) It involved the murder of a young woman. In the subsequent trial a policeman, referring to the facts of the case, stated in evidence that, 'The body of the woman had been decapitated and dismembered, but there was no evidence that she had been interfered with.'

I have a story of my own which I have recounted many times and which contains an example of ludicrous but rather endearing euphemism that only the British Army could have conceived.

The scene was Wellington Barracks in London in the mid-forties. One day, the Regimental Sergeant-Major in my wartime regiment, the Grenadier Guards, left his quarters shortly after dawn, and set off across the barrack square like a man-o'-war in full sail to carry out his morning inspection. In the middle of the square, his eye fell upon what in army regulations was known as a 'nuisance', standing proud and defiant on the tarmac. Finding a culprit, he had him up before his company commander later that same morning. (As a junior officer, I stood with others behind the colonel, trying to keep a straight face.) The soldier gave as his excuse that, on the way back from the pub the previous night, he had been taken short. At this point the RSM interrupted, using the archaic form of words demanded by King's Regulations. 'I thank you, sir, for leave to speak!' The colonel nodded. 'I myself examined the nuisance with my pace-stick and found it 'ard and hobviously made with heffort!'

I tend to be Soperish (a short pause here while I persuade my computer's spell-check that 'Soperish' is OK) about the most notorious four-letter word, except in moments of extreme anger or frustration. Anglo-Saxon or not, it sounds to me ugly, brutish and aggressive. When used frequently and indiscriminately, it loses all point, becoming no more than a rather distressing speech impediment. There are times, on the other hand, when it too can be indispensable and euphemism-proof.

When I worked on the London *Daily Mail* as a cartoonist in the late forties, I shared a room with the photo toucher-uppers.

Artists in their own way, they would in those days edit photographs using grey paint and cotton buds to remove unwanted backgrounds or, in the case of close-ups, facial blemishes. In charge of them was a mild, middle-aged man called Claude, who did his work perched on a high stool like a Dickensian bookkeeper.

Among his team was a tall, leery, shark-faced man called Ted, with black, patent-leather hair and an evil grin, whose primary aim was to give Claude as hard a time as possible. One day, having worked the morning shift, Ted went off to lunch at one o'clock. Meanwhile, Claude came in for the afternoon shift and, believing that Ted was on the same shift, mildly rebuked him on his return for coming in late. 'Late?' said Ted in exaggerated outrage, 'Whadyer mean, late? I've been 'ere since the-fuckin'-smornin'!'

The next example invites a somewhat longer build-up. When my friend and colleague tenor saxist Jimmy Skidmore died in 1998, the Order of Service at his funeral bore on the front, under his name and photograph, not the conventional RIP but, in bold letters, the initials KYBL.

The first time I became aware of the significance of those initials in Jimmy's life was in 1948, the year of the First International Jazz Festival in Nice. He and I were there as members of an *ad hoc* (in modern lingo, 'pick-up') British band which joined the cast of American and European musicians headed by Louis Armstrong.

The Nice Festival was a significant event as at least fifteen years had elapsed since Louis Armstrong had last crossed the Atlantic. (He hadn't appeared in England since 1933.) His arrival at the Festival was akin to the return of a conquering hero. Most of the cast had arrived in Nice before him and we all attended an official reception in the Town Hall to welcome him. The huge room was packed and there was a great roar of conversation as we awaited his arrival.

I remember that moment well. Even before Louis came into the room, the familiar gruff voice, thanks to its timbre and pitch, cut through the excited hubbub. After applause and speeches, he was eventually brought over to a table at which some of us were already queuing to shake his hand and mumble a few words of welcome. Jimmy Skidmore was ahead of me in the queue and I watched as he reached the table, shook Louis Armstrong's hand and bent forward to say something to him. I couldn't hear what he said, but it was received with a guttural burst of laughter. When I had paid homage myself, I caught up with Jimmy and asked him what had so amused Armstrong. 'I just said, "Kiss your bum later,"' was his answer.

It may be deduced from this that Jimmy Skidmore was what the guardian of my childhood years, Nanny Viggers, used to call a 'caution'. He was a dear man, who showed me great kindness when I started working on the London jazz scene as an amateur. In the late fifties, he joined my band, and for five years or so enlivened its existence with fine tenor saxophone playing and a nervy ebullience which was rarely short of outrageous but never ill-intended. With his vigorous crop of sprouting black hair, lined face, glass-shattering voice and formidable dental equipment clearly intended by the Creator for a horse, he was not someone whose presence in a room could be ignored.

Jimmy was still a member of my band in 1959 when I wrote (in my book, *Second Chorus*, published by McGibbon and Kee), 'his spiritual ancestry goes back to the era of music hall, of cheery banter and cheeky backchat. Even in the most demure company he will express himself in quite uninhibited terms – and then dispel the shock with a huge, tusky grin which says, "Don't mind me, ducks – I don't mean half I say."'

On stage, Jimmy's noisy interjections and irrepressible humour were not always welcomed by his fellow musicians. We were once playing a late concert in a cinema in Bedford after the film programme had finished. Jimmy was unable to pass up the opportunity for mayhem offered by the spotlit silver screen behind us. Joe Temperley, at one point playing a lyrical solo on baritone saxophone, was bewildered to hear gusts of laughter from the audience. He didn't know that Skidmore was creating hand silhouettes of ducks and rabbits on the screen behind him.

I suffered a similar fate a few years after Jimmy had left my band, when he and I were booked as guests with Harry Stoneham's trio at a jazz pub in South London.

The layout of the Plough at Stockwell offered Jimmy a field day of outrageousness. The route to the ladies' toilet passed alongside the low bandstand, and visitors to it would run the gauntlet of a battery of familiar 'Skidmore-isms'. It would be, 'Mention my name and you'll get a good seat!' on their way in and, worse still, 'Could you hear us, darlin'? 'Cos we could hear you!' on the way out. When he and I played there, he was in the throes of breaking in a new set of lower-jaw dentures, which made blowing the saxophone uncomfortable. I was in the middle of playing what might well have been my best-ever solo on Duke Ellington's 'In A Mellotone' when the laughter started. A quick check on the trouser-zip eliminated the only possible reason for the irreverent mirth that I could conceive, so I soldiered on to the end of the solo, then turned to Jimmy for enlightenment. His bottom set of false teeth was draped over his left ear.

On most occasions, the conciliatory 'Don't mind me, darlin'' turned aside wrath, one exception being an occasion in New York when he addressed it to a cop who had pulled him up for jaywalking. In seconds he was up against a wall with legs akimbo and the cop's nightstick seriously threatening his dignity, if nothing else. As his bandleader, I took most of the excesses in my stride.

Jimmy was, in age and experience, senior to me, and sometimes played the old soldier. He was the sole inventor of what I dubbed the Skidmore Watch, a timepiece which contrived to be five minutes slow when a concert was due to start and five minutes fast by the time we approached the end, at which point he would tap it pointedly as I prepared to announce a final number.

When he joined my band, he was suffering from a stomach ulcer, and could drink only Harvey's Dry Sherry. After a perforation put him in hospital for a month or two, he emerged ulcer-free, rejoined the band and set about making up for lost time. On occasion whisky got the better of him and the results were spectacular. The story I have to tell involves swearing on a grandiloquent scale, but cannot be euphemised.

When we played in Glasgow in the fifties, it was customary for us to go after the show to the house of Norman McSwan, a distinguished heart surgeon at Ruchill Hospital, an ardent jazz enthusiast and a good friend to musicians. There we would join his wife Margaret and some of their friends for a late night cup of tea. After a short while, the friends would take their leave and Margaret would say, 'Well, I'll be away to my bed.' Then the tea would be replaced by a bottle or two of Scotch and we would settle in for the rest of the night to listen to records and, as Norrie's generous libations took their toll, become more or less incoherent.

After one of these sessions, our trombonist John Picard, still admirably in some control of his senses, undertook the task of helping an incapacitated Jimmy Skidmore back to the hotel. It was early dawn and we had to prepare almost immediately to leave for Prestwick Airport to catch a flight back to London. John packed Jimmy's case and saxophone and, when the time came, got them and him on to the coach.

At the airport, after checking in, we went to the cafeteria to await the call and, with the aid of black coffee, managed to induce in Jimmy some signs of life. It was not altogether a wise move. The room had filled up with passengers, most of them prim-looking Scottish mothers with wide-eyed offspring in tow, perhaps heading for school in England. Returning to something like consciousness, Jimmy's first thought was for his saxophone, with which he had lost touch. John reassured him that everything had been taken care of, and he was duly grateful. Looking across the table, he mumbled, 'What a friend . . .'

There was an ominous pause. Many people in their lives have experienced a vivid moment of presentiment just before some disaster has occurred. Sitting round the table, we all held our breath. Then, outrageousness having seeped back along with his other faculties, Jimmy turned to the assembled company and trumpeted, 'What a FU–U–U–U–UCKIN' friend!'

There I will leave Jimmy Skidmore with the valediction RIP or perhaps, if it turns out that there is life after death, KYBL.

*

For anyone inclined to be prudish, difficulty arises when, in the interests of euphemism, perfectly harmless words acquire a double entendre.

Once, when we played at a public school in Dorset, my band was invited by the Headmaster and his wife to join them and a few friends and helpers for a light supper before the concert. We sat round a large dining-room table eating chicken and salad. I was placed next to the Head's wife, with our then bass player, Paul Bridge, a ready laugher, on her other side. In the course of the conversation, she said that she had heard my band play many years earlier at a May Ball at Oxford. At that point, as often happens at dinner tables, the general chatter petered out and, in the brief silence, she turned to me and asked 'Do you still play a lot of balls?' Paul had just taken a large mouthful of salad and the ensuing explosion was seismic.

It used to be the custom, in polite society, to disguise utterances of a dubious nature by translating them into a foreign language, usually French. '*Pas devant les domestiques,*' was the phrase used by hostesses at dinner-parties to deflect anecdotes that might offend or startle those waiting at table – whose own language below stairs would probably have scorched the cutlery, but no matter. Sometimes, using a foreign language itself can be hazardous if the speaker is unsure or ignorant of its meaning. Buck Clayton, one of the great jazz trumpeters, toured several times with my band and became a close friend. It was he who told me this cautionary tale.

Buck Clayton was in France with a band that included the American tenor saxophonist Don Byas, who at that time lived in Holland. When they played at the home town of their pianist, André Persianny, he invited them all for a meal at the house of his parents. In the taxi on the way, Buck suggested to Don Byas that they should perhaps buy a bunch of flowers for their hostess. Byas told him that, on the Continent, it was considered more complimentary to offer just a single rose, to which Buck agreed. He spoke no French so, on the way from the flower shop, he got Don, who was fluent, to suggest a few suitable words in French to accompany the presentation. Don obliged, and Buck duly memorised and rehearsed them during the rest of the journey.

When they arrived at the house, Madame Persianny was at the door to greet them. Holding out the rose on its prickly stalk, he delivered the prepared speech, and was disconcerted when she turned pale, then puce, and fled from the room. As André Persianny ushered them hurriedly out into the street Buck turned to Don for an explanation, to find him convulsed with malicious laughter.

I will leave readers to supply their own indelicate punchlines, being, as listeners to *I'm Sorry I Haven't A Clue* will know, an innocent in these matters.

I am told, by persons whose comments and opinions I trust, that the scripts for that BBC Radio 4 panel-game with which I am furnished by a brilliant comic scriptwriter, Iain Pattinson, are riddled with innuendo and double entendre. There are, indeed, occasions when some harmless line I have read from a card is greeted by uproarious and somewhat crude laughter from the audience. I am not offended by this, believing that, in this harsh and competitive life, any sign of appreciation is welcome. Indeed, I was flattered a few years ago when the *Sunday Telegraph Magazine* had me, inexplicably, in a list of 'One Hundred National Treasures', including in the citation the words 'jazz trumpeter, broadcaster and [the capitals are mine] Purveyor of Blue Chip Filth to Middle England.' For a brief moment I thought of buying a small white van to have those words emblazoned under my name on the side, but I have enough parallel careers to cope with already.

As for the Buck Clayton experience, I did once unknowingly inflict on an innocent party a cruel joke along the Don Byas line. In 1957, my band did a weekly series of fifteen-minute TV programmes for Granada Television. The company was then in its early days. The studios and offices were housed in a clutch of single-storey buildings and it seemed to us that the atmosphere was heavily suffused with a certain rakish glamour.

Our show, entitled *Here's Humph,* went out 'live' at 6.45 p.m. on Fridays, from a studio set simulating a jazz club in which the audience was encouraged to dance. We would take the 9.30 a.m. train from Euston to Manchester, arriving at Granada in time for lunch and a desultory afternoon rehearsal. On arrival the first time, we were pleasantly surprised to find on a table in the band's dressing room an array of bottles – whisky, gin, wine and beer, together with all the necessary accompaniments. It has to be said, in passing, that there were occasions when, as an announcer's voice boomed, 'It's 6.45 and here's Humph!' we went 'on air' with no more than a fingertip's grasp of reality.

One Friday, during the gap between rehearsal and show, one of the make-up girls, a big girl called Jenny, full of warmth and laughter, came into the dressing room and asked if anyone could speak Welsh. Having spent long family holidays in Harlech, North Wales, between 1929 and the outbreak of World War II, I had picked up a phrase or two, mostly from a woman who cooked for us in a succession of rented houses. She had a mischievous sense of humour, and taught me till I was pronunciation-perfect a sentence the meaning of which she refused to divulge, saying no more than, 'You'll find out one day!' The phrase '*Damia cathray*

HL circa 1930, at the Babraham Hall home farm, discovering with a sickly grin that an equestrian life was not for him.

At thirteen, wearing a duffed-up version of the Eton College school uniform.

Heavily outnumbered at home with, left to right, sisters Diana, Helena, Rose and Mary.

THE BRIGADE OF GUARDS 1941

Back in uniform. HL, left, with three fellow recruits at Caterham Barracks. On the right, Trained Soldier Standerline, in charge of us. I don't know what he had to smile about?

Mission accomplished! 2nd Lieutenant Lyttelton standing behind HRH Princess Elizabeth, who is doing her best to look like a Colonel-in-Chief of the Regiment.

Cartoonist on the *Daily Mail*, 1947, with pen poised over blank sheet of paper in the hope that an idea will occur.

In action in the London Jazz Club, Piccadilly, 1948. The cornetist trying to blow me offstage was American visitor Jimmy McPartland. Envious of the beard?

Asked to smile for the camera, we say 'cheese'. Louis Armstrong has just said 'spaghetti'!

In 100 Oxford Street, 1958. People asked why I played with my eyes shut? Wouldn't you, under Jimmy Rushing's critical look?

Photo call at the Marquee Club, 1958. The photographer has just said 'Look as if you're playing something'. In dark suits, left to right, John Picard, Brian Brocklehurst, Jimmy Skidmore, Tony Coe, Eddie Taylor, Joe Temperley.

In Dubai, 1979. John Barnes (left) with Bruce Turner, who is probably squeaking.

On *I'm Sorry I Haven't a Clue* in the seventies. Chairman Humph in (rare) genial mode.

Humph cartoons drawn for the *Daily Mail*, circa 1950:

1) 'And when you take the clocks down to put them forward, don't forget to put them back!'

2) 'It's the same every year – and he *still* calls it "seeing the New Year in"!'

3) 'You should be Chancellor of the Exchequer – you can free a pound quicker than anyone I know.' (Note: This was a topical reference to the then Chancellor of the Exchequer, R A Butler, and his plan to 'free the pound' from international currency restrictions.)

4) 'I think we'd better leave your father until Twelfth Night, too.'

The *Clue* team in a bout of rare athleticism. Left to right: Barry Cryer, Graeme Garden, Willie Rushton, Tim Brooke-Taylor.

Abstract. Painted by Luuk Add, an artist in Thailand (see pp 159–60).

Into Oldham. Watercolour by Robert Littleford, Oldham artist.

Section of the audience for the Radiohead concert in South Park, Oxford, 2001, photographed by a trembling Diamond Geezer about to go onstage.

diawl' has stayed with me ever since, shrouded in mystery until very recently.

Certainly, I had no idea what it meant when I offered it to Jenny, asking at the same time why she needed it. She explained that she had, waiting for her in the make-up chair, the Archbishop of Llandaff, who was to be interviewed in a discussion programme going out immediately after ours in another studio. She thought that a little bit of Welsh might impress him. After a bit of hasty coaching, she had memorised my little phrase sufficiently to hurry back to her Archbishop. It was when we were packing up our instruments after our show that she came into the studio, her normally sunny expression eclipsed by what was obviously deep distress. 'What on earth did you tell me to say to the Archbishop?' she shouted. I said, 'I have no idea, it was just a bit of Welsh. Why, what happened?'

She described, with much agitated heaving of her ample breast, how, halfway through the application of the quite heavy make-up required by TV in those days, she had leant forward and murmured *'Damia cathray diawl'* into the prelate's ear, hoping for a surprised but genial response. The Archbishop rose to his feet, snatched the protective towel from his shoulders and stormed out of the make-up room, subsequently to appear for his interview with one half of his face enhanced with Pancake make-up, the other *au naturel.*

It was many decades later, while recording an *I'm Sorry I Haven't A Clue* show programme in Rhyl, that I discovered from the theatre manager that the sweet nothings I had given the poor girl to breath into the Archbishop's ear mean, 'Damn you and go to the Devil!'

I have to confess that, having stored that Welsh phrase for so many years in a memory file labelled 'Rude words', I was disappointed to find it so inoffensive – to anyone, that is, barring the then Archishop of Llandaff.

*

91

Once or twice in the past pages I have strayed nervously into the realms of high technology. It's a subject of which people of advanced age, I have discovered, are assumed to be totally ignorant, as they are of practically everything else in modern life. The early signs of this assumption appear when one takes a handful of loose change out of the trouser pocket – to pay for, say, a newspaper or a bar of chocolate – to find one's wrist seized in an iron grip by the zealous shop-assistant who then proceeds to pick the appropriate coins from the palm of one's hand, muttering the while such empty phrases as 'There you go' in a soothing voice. I'm not given to cannibalism, but on these occasions I have to resist the primordial urge to sink my teeth into the offender's own invasive wrist.

Having, as a recording musician, lived from the era of wax discs in the forties to the digital wizardry of today, I have had perforce to absorb at least a surface awareness of advancing technology, while retaining a healthy scepticism that can be expressed in a brace of thoughts.

'Progress' is Nature's way of reconciling the elderly to the prospect of death.

Chairman Humph in ruminative mode

That is not, I think, an idiosyncratic notion. Many people who have listened – perhaps on the BBC Radio 4 *Today* programme – to some scientist predicting that computers will eventually usurp almost every activity of the human brain, will have shared with me the thought 'Not in my lifetime, thank goodness!'

I was once booked to give an after-dinner speech to the regional heads of department for IBM. As often happens on these occasions, the company chairman spoke first and proved a hard act to follow. Having been upstaged in that way, I have since felt no guilt in purloining his most successful story.

In a pub near IBM's offices in Hammersmith, to which many of the company's employees would pop out for lunch, there was a regular who was an avowed computerphobe. Perched on a stool at the bar, he noisily aired his belief that the machines could do nothing that couldn't be accomplished more quickly by pen and paper. The IBM people got so fed up with his constant sniping while they were eating their ploughman's lunch that they invited him to their showrooms to see for himself what state-of-the-art computers could do. When he continued to scoff, they took him to a room that housed a top-secret model not yet revealed to the public. They explained to the sceptical Luddite that it could answer on the monitor screen any question put to it verbally. When he guffawed in disbelief, they challenged him to ask it a question.

After a little thought he said, with a cunning look, 'Where is my father now?' Within seconds the answer came up: 'Your father is on the golf course at Sunningdale.' He turned to them with a look of triumph. 'There you are – I told you they're a load of rubbish. My father's been dead for four years!' Hardly had he turned back to the screen when the words came up, 'No, the man who married your mother has been dead for four years. Your father is on the golf course at Sunningdale.'

What is the relevance of this anecdote? Only that when I once told it to someone well versed in matters hi-tech, he maintained a straight face and solemnly observed that such an all-knowing computer is perfectly conceivable and may already exist on the drawing-board. Unbridled enthusiasm for such developments is strictly for the young, the not-so-young having the responsibility to utter words of caution.

> Almost all good ideas, given time, will turn out to have been bad ideas.
>
> Chairman Humph in sceptical mode

Jon Naismith, our inspired producer on *I'm Sorry I Haven't A Clue*, has a tendency to book us all, on out-of-town broadcasts, into state-of-the-art, high-tech hotels of which decor, furnishings and fittings are of a kind that fill the glossy 'style' magazines – and indeed were effectively lampooned in the hilarious Jacques Tati film *Mon Oncle*. During a recent series, we found ourselves in one such hotel on the South Coast. Because the people running it did their friendly best to welcome us, I will mention neither the hotel's name nor its location. I reckon its gadgets and flummeries alone, if not replaced, will put it out of business soon enough without any help from me.

The first thing that struck me when I was shown into my room was the bath. It stood, surprisingly, in the bedroom itself, within an arm's reach of the bed, a huge white tub in which, at six-foot, two-and-a-half inches in my stockinged feet, I could happily have reclined full length and had space to execute a few graceful backstrokes. What prevented me from achieving this luxury was the fact that the bath, at least two-and-a-half feet deep, was mounted on a foot-high red plinth. To get into it would have demanded some basic training in mountaineering. To get out of it would have required the assistance of the fire-brigade. As a finishing touch, there was a potted plant perched on one end, its long bare stem crowned by a few delicate white blooms of some exotic variety. One false move in all the floundering-about would tip a potful of soil into the water. The sight of the whole ludicrous edifice would surely have prompted even the Rev. Donald Soper to suspend his aversion to the word 'bullshit'.

Why, you may be asking yourselves, was the bath in the bedroom? The answer is, because there was no place for it in the 'wet-room'. Wet-rooms are those that have a shower in the ceiling, a plughole in the floor and gently sloping floor-tiles that drain away the water. Described thus simply, it seems a good idea. No stepping gingerly into a slithery cubicle, no fiddling with a reluctant plastic curtain to keep it inside the shower as instructed. Just get undressed, walk into the room, turn on a tap on the wall and – whoosh!

The trouble is, a wet-room is a luxury that few cramped, terraced seaside promenade hotels can easily accommodate. Our ultra-modern establishment faced the problem head-on by putting the washbasin, the WC and other facilities in the same space, thus laying the foundation for a compendium of rotten ideas. Before the shower was unleashed, all towels, hastily discarded pyjamas, dressing gowns, toilet-bags, even loo-paper, had to be removed. The guest going in fully dressed to wash the hands before going down to breakfast or out on the town, had only to turn a wrong tap to be thoroughly dowsed in water. Iain Pattinson, our scriptwriter, was not amused when he pulled a string hanging from the ceiling, which he thought would turn on the light, and brought the entire hotel staff rushing to his room in the belief that he was a disabled person in need of help. In another room, our guest on the programme, the glum-faced comedian, Jack Dee, finding that his designer loo wouldn't flush properly, took the designer lid off the designer cistern to investigate and it slipped from his wet fingers on to the designer tiles, shattering into a hundred designer pieces.

All this happened before my arrival, providing a prologue to what I can only describe as a far-fetched Keystone comedy routine, or perhaps a Monsieur Hulot episode discarded by Jacques Tati as being too over-the-top.

Jon Naismith had come to the door of my room at 6 p.m. to tell me that the taxis taking us to the theatre for the evening performance were waiting outside. I called out to him that I was all ready, then popped in to the wet-room to wash my hands. The washbasin tap was a cleverly contrived all-in-one masterpiece of industrial design, a single fitting that responded to a few deft movements comparable to those required to open a safe – a forward tilt to start the flow, a twist here to adjust the temperature, a turn there to control the jet.

My initial manoeuvre turned on the water at full jet, the pressure of which blew the entire elongated spout from the wall with a force that bounced it off my midriff back into the basin. Water gushed unrestrained from the exposed hole in the wall. Like the little Dutch boy of legend, I quick-wittedly jabbed my right thumb on to the breach in the dam, partially stemming the flow while I shouted to my producer outside the door to fetch help. It's not easy to remain ice-cool on these occasions and it was a few seconds before it occurred to me to turn off the tap. To do this, I had to reach across with my left hand – the one, since I am right-handed, least ready for split-second response. In its desperate fumbling it turned the complex mechanism the wrong way, further increasing the jet. The water arrogantly swept aside my thumb and, with a surge that almost took my hand off at the wrist, drenched me in a second from head to foot, from jacket to skin, from carefully adjusted tie to colour-coordinated socks. For a final touch, part of the cataract passed over my head and shoulders to soak the bed behind me and water the pot plant on the rim of the bath. With nothing further to lose, I fought my way upstream to turn off the tap, then turned still dripping copiously to the door just as Jon Naismith and a posse from Reception arrived to see what all the shouting was about.

As I changed hurriedly into dry clothes, an apt thought presented itself:

Today's disaster is tomorrow's anecdote.

Chairman Humph in soggy mode

A reader of acute perception will have grasped that I am not completely at home with hi-tech. When I bought my first computer in the eighties, I was appalled to discover how soon I started to talk to it. It used to be said that talking to oneself was the first sign of madness. Surely talking to one's computer falls into the same diagnostic category. When, in response to an e-mail, I lingered in thought and was told sternly, 'You have been idle too long,' my spontaneous reaction was to say out loud, 'Oooh, sorry,

sorry!' a knee-jerk response no doubt triggered by the distant memory of schooldays, when I was only too familiar with that reprimand. When I got to know the computer a bit better, I became more assertive, uttering a testy 'C'mon, C'mON!' as it dawdled through the lengthy process of booting up. (Booting up? It should have been me doing the booting up.) I'm bound to say that computer programmers seem to me singularly tactless. Nobody wants to be accused, in their own home, of performing an illegal operation, and the brutal diagnosis 'Fatal Error' might well put someone of a nervous disposition into intensive care.

*

Talking of silliness, which we were seemingly weeks ago, this story was told to me by the British jazz pianist Lenny Felix at three o'clock in the morning in the Lyons Corner House, Tottenham Court Road (ah yes, you could do things like that in the bad old post-war days). I have put the narrative into my own words.

Lennie, known then by his real name, Lennie Jacobus, worked in a small radio station in India in the immediate post-war years. An Indian producer booked him to top the bill in a broadcast variety show. At rehearsal during the day, the man, who was also the show's compère, appeared immaculate in white suit, with hair sleeked back and head full of grandiose ideas. These he outlined to the motley cast with much reference to his show-business experience and distinction. One of those ideas was that, for the high spot of the show, he would announce Lennie with the words, 'And now, ladies and gentlemen, the wizard of the keyboard, Lennie J . . . A . . . C . . . O . . . B . . . U . . . S!' requiring the pianist to play a crashing chord after each letter.

After rehearsal, the cast dispersed for a long break. On their return, they were greeted by an apparition with white suit crumpled, hair dishevelled and the voice of authority slurred and barely articulate. Somehow, at the appointed time, the live broadcast started and lurched along precariously until the time came for the star of the show to be announced. The compère/producer having, as drunks do, worked on the principle that matters would be improved by further recourse to the bottle, was by then totally smashed. In all circumstances, of course, the show must go on. Peering fruitlessly at his clipboard, the man embarked on the prepared introduction.

'Annow, laids an' ge'men, the wzzd of the keyboar', Lennie J . . .' (dutiful crash on the piano) '. . . V . . .' (rather more hesitant crash, followed by a prolonged pause and heavy breathing) '. . . Six . . .' (even longer pause, at the end of which Mr Showbusiness shrugged his shoulders and collapsed, stupefied, into a chair). Lennie, aborting a third crash in mid-descent, launched into his set without further ceremony and continued until the red studio light signalled the end of the show.

*

We have reached a rather giddy stage in this book when subjects will start to spin on their heels through 360 degrees without any warning. At some point in my early life, I memorised a passage that for many years I assumed came from P G Wodehouse. When, some years ago, the BBC invited me to present a programme in a series about humour, I wanted to include it as a personal choice, but was unable to use it because nobody, including some Wodehouse experts, was able to confirm for copyright purposes that he had written it. I have to ask, who else could it be?

The passage concerns a young man called Ffinch who travels to a big country house in the Home Counties to dine with an American tycoon from whom he hopes to get a job. After the meal, the American takes him to the library for an interview. The interview starts unpromisingly when the tycoon, who has punished the port severely, takes a fountain pen from his breast pocket, puts it in his mouth and applies a match to it. It is he who starts the conversation. It must be read slowly, with impeccable timing:

'Are you married, Winch?'

'Ffinch.'

'How d' you mean, Ffinch?

'My name is Ffinch.'

'What of it?'

'You called me Winch.'

'Why?'

'I suppose you thought it was my name.'

'What was?'

'Winch.'

'But you said just now it was Ffinch.'

'So it is.'

'Look here, young man, enough of this shilly-shallying. Let your yea be yea and your nay be nay. If your name is Pinch, speak it out like a man!'

They say that the Italian painter Giotto was able to draw a perfect circle freehand, without using a compass. I once gained the information from somewhere that the great pioneer of the oboe, Leon Goossens, learned from glass-blowers the technique of circular breathing, by which air can be expelled from the mouth and, simultaneously, taken in through the nostrils to sustain an unbroken note almost indefinitely. Circular dialogue such as the passage above impresses me just as much, and I wish I had written it myself. At least I can report a spontaneous example, oft told.

Years ago, on the outskirts of Bradford, I took part, with an elderly and irascible passer-by, in the following verbal *pas de deux*. Mine was the opening move. Pulling up alongside him, I wound the passenger window down and leaned across.

'Excuse me, can you tell me the way to Bradford University?'

'Bradford University? There isn't one.'

Believing him to be hard of hearing, I raised my voice, repeating myself in the process.

'Yes there is. Bradford University . . . Bradford University . . . (crescendo) I'M LOOKING FOR BRADFORD UNIVERSITY!"

'THERE ISN'T ONE!'

'THERE MUST BE ONE – I'M GOING TO A CONCERT THERE TONIGHT!'

'WELL, WHERE IS IT, THEN?'

As one further example of the circular genre, I recall a little gem from an old edition of *Punch* magazine.

The cartoon was by George Belcher. Like many of the Punch artists of his generation, he was more of an illustrator than a cartoonist in the modern sense. His charcoal drawings often featured what used to be called charladies. In the cartoon in question, it's a sturdy member of that noble profession who stands in the centre of the picture, holding a feather duster and looking disconsolately at the ruins of a large vase that has fallen from a pedestal. She addresses the dismayed lady of the house who surveys the scene from the doorway:

Charlady: 'Oh, ma'am, when I seen what I done, I sez to meself, Good Lord, what 'ave you done?'

In the history of wordplay, that caption is timeless.

Another thought has occurred, prompted by I know not what. Perhaps the keyword is silliness.

Youthful shyness is never outgrown. It's just that, as we grow older, we learn how to handle it better.

Chairman Humph in philosophical mode

I don't think I have completely mastered how to handle it yet. Certainly I was well into adulthood when I took a small step in the direction of becoming a London clubman. Stationed near London in 1946, while waiting for demob from the army, I was invited many times by a fellow officer and great friend, Hugo Charteris, to join him for lunch at his club, the Travellers.

Hugo, who later became a writer and died at a ridiculously early age, was a man after my own heart, rebellious about army life and even scruffier on parade than myself. This was largely due to his ownership of a large and friendly golden retriever that would chew anything it could close its teeth on, being particularly fond of the leather belt and cap-band which his batman laid out on the bed before a prestigious parade.

After several of our lunches together, Hugo suggested to me that I should join the Travellers Club myself. I went along with that, and he duly sponsored my candidature. Nobody blackballed me, so I was elected, receiving a warm letter of welcome from the secretary. When it came to breezing in there on my own, a new boy amongst all those strangers ensconced in their leather-bound armchairs and on the lookout for any breach of etiquette, I postponed the moment. It has remained postponed until this day.

I once described myself as 'unclubbable', the word social workers used to apply to loutish youths who hang about on street corners instead of joining youth clubs. There have been exceptions. In childhood, I was a 'Gugnunc'. I'll move to a new paragraph now to let that momentous announcement sink in.

Gugnunc was the name of a club associated with the *Daily Mirror* strip-cartoon called 'Pip, Squeak and Wilfred' which, alas, few people now remember. (Things have come to a pretty pass when you can't ring up a friend and discuss the latest episode. Strip cartoons were the soap operas of their day.) So I have to explain that Pip was a hearty dog of the mongrel variety, Squeak was a sleek penguin and Wilfred was a hyperactive rabbit. There were other supporting characters – Squeak had a relative called for quite obvious reasons

Auntie, who was also a penguin, but hairy. I have never seen a hairy penguin, but if David Attenborough keeps at it, one is bound to turn up sooner or later. There was also Popski, a canine anarchist (I hope you're riveted by all this), who provided a bit of suspense by never being seen without one of those spherical bombs with spluttering fuses that used to identify anarchists in cartoons.

I seem to recall that Wilfred tended to hog the show, speaking with a limited vocabulary of monosyllables – Ick, Goo, Boo, Par and Nunc, the latter suggesting a classical education. These were assembled into the passwords by which members of the Gugnuncs identified each other. The idea was that one would confront someone in the street with the challenge 'Ick, Ick, Par, Boo!' They would, if they belonged to said club, respond with 'Goo, Goo, Par, Nunc!' and brotherhood would be established. Non-members would identify themselves by walking quickly away, trying not to break into a run, while looking round anxiously for a policeman. (I think I may have left some details out, but never mind, you get the gist.)

It was only in very recent times that I discovered, when I had almost abandoned hope, that one of the little team with whom I lunch regularly in local pubs was once a Gugnunc. Now, I and Leo Gibbons-Smith, a distinguished artist, former president of the United Society of Artists and fellow octogenarian, quite often exchange those passwords when we meet in the pub, while the regulars at the bar exchange meaningful glances, their previous assumptions confirmed.

I don't think I would ever have been a keen practising Gugnunc. As a child, I was agonisingly shy. It was due to the wild terror of being confronted by strangers that I once set fire to a vicar. His name, suitably enough in this context, was Popham and he was the parent of a boy in my father's House at Eton.

The fourth of June was what most people would describe as an 'open day' at Eton College. Parents would converge on the school, fathers to relive their own schooldays; mothers, in their finery and outrageous hats, to watch proudly as their embarrassed offspring took part in events that went on through the day. It all culminated in a firework display which itself ended with the National Anthem and a sparkling and spluttering pyrotechnical representation of George V and Queen Mary. It was during one such day that I, as a small boy, unwittingly staged a small firework event of my own.

Wandering about the house, I was suddenly confronted by a total stranger in clerical garb, who had walked in through the open front door of Warre House to see my father. Not knowing how to deal with the situation, I charged at him playfully and butted him in the midriff, whereupon he burst into flames. Appalled, I turned and fled while he slapped frenetically at his waistcoat. In medieval times, I might have earned some notoriety as a precocious agent of the Devil. The cause was, I'm afraid, more mundane. He had in his waistcoat pocket a box of non-safety Swan Vestas matches that the impact of my head had ignited.

Shyness overcame me, more embarrassingly, on my first day at Sunningdale School, the still-flourishing family-run boarding school to which I was consigned at the age of eight.

My parents had driven me there and handed me over to the headmaster, Mr Crabtree. He and his wife assembled all the new boys in their drawing room to welcome us to the school. The nervous trauma of having just seen my father's car disappearing down the winding drive, and then finding myself in the middle of a lot of strange, chattering boys who appeared to have made friends already, manifested itself in the increasingly urgent demands of my bladder. Too shy to interrupt the headmaster's welcoming speech and ask where the loo was, I burst into tears and simultaneously peed on the carpet. I remember a fellow new boy, clearly not destined for the diplomatic corps in later life, crying, 'Look, he's dripping!'

I have never since subscribed to the notion that it helps to build the character of eight-year-old children by taking them from home and dumping them ('maroon' was the appropriate word in my case) in a strange place among strangers without so much as a goodbye or farewell embrace. It was done with the best of intentions. I have no doubt that, as they pulled away from the school gates, my father comforted my mother with, 'Don't worry – he'll be playing happily with new-found friends already.' If so, he was whistling in the wind. For several terms, the dreadful bouts of homesickness recurred – the apprehensive counting of days as the end of the holidays approached, the journey on the day in the family car (a 'tumbril' to me) and the subsequent nocturnal sobbing under the blankets in the cubicle or dormitory. To avoid the upset that the parting caused them, my parents took to delegating the job of driving me to school to Mr Vickery the odd-job man who, apart from occasionally muttering the contradictory words, 'Come on, lad, be a man' from beneath a moustache of Lord Kitchener proportions, was able to remain calmly detached throughout the journey.

Many years later, when I was a parent myself, I drove one hundred and fifty miles to deliver our then eight-year-old son Stephen to a sort of country-house camp in Wiltshire organised by a fellow-parent at his school in North London. It would have been his first extended absence from home and, though there were a few friends of his there, a crescendo of heavy sighs from the passenger seat of the car indicated that he was not ready for the experience.

When we arrived, the clouds of apprehension burst. It reached a point at which the hosts suggested that the only way to stop the uncontrollable sobbing was for me to hop in my car and drive off, and that he would 'soon be playing happily with new-found friends'. It was that moment, echoing my own experience on my first day at Sunningdale, that persuaded me there and then to take him to the car and drive us both one hundred and fifty miles home. With chickenpox, glandular fever, tonsillitis, croup, scarlet fever, mumps and two kinds of measles then on the menu of childhood ailments, I didn't think it was necessary to add homesickness.

To put the record straight, I should add that the tears rolled when, after four years, it was time to leave Sunningdale. My days there did have a profound influence on my future life, if not my character. After a year or two, Mr Crabtree retired, to be replaced by Geoffrey Dacre Fox. It would be hard to find two men less alike in both appearance and style. Where Crabtree was crumpled and grizzly, prone to outbursts of temper and a ferocious wielder of the cane, Fox was sleek and unruffled, from the black hair, dark and glossy as patent leather and greased flat, down to the ample plus-fours and the co-respondent shoes. Crabtree's academic stance was, broadly speaking, classical, and Fox's more open to modern ideas. When he took over as Headmaster, the latter continued the practice of reading to the assembled School on Sunday mornings, but the story he chose was more likely to be from the adventures of Bulldog Drummond than Barnaby Rudge.

I do however also recall Shakespeare readings in his drawing room on other occasions. As usual, something quite silly has kept it in my mind.

The memory is of Mr Fox sitting on a chair with the group of boys sprawling round him on the carpet, each clutching a softback school edition of the play in question. He used to allocate to us the various roles in the scene. Once, the play was *Richard II*, in which appear three servants to the king: Bushy, Bagot and Green. One of our group was a boy called Brunel (I forget his first name) who was the great grandson, I believe, of the great engineer, Isambard Kingdom Brunel.

It is well known to be a bad career move for a schoolboy, especially in the early days of school life, to stand out from the crowd. Poor Brunel had a bad time, largely due to his hair, a prodigious black growth that sprouted above his ears at all angles like some sort of ill-conceived winter headgear. Mr Fox was a sympathetic man. I am sure it was with no malicious intent that he caused a minor riot with the announcement, 'Brunel, you will be Bushy.'

Similarly, I doubt if Geoffrey Fox had any notion of the effect it would have on my life when he modernised the annual school concerts. With his encouragement, they became more like variety shows, drawing on talent that had hitherto been regarded, if at all, as inadmissibly lowbrow. I benefited from this on two scores. Noticing my habit of scribbling fanciful doodles all over my school books and, indeed, any other blank surface that offered itself, he got me to channel the destructive tendency into a form of entertainment then known as Lightning Cartoons (nowadays occasionally resurrected on television in various forms). If I feel in the mood for a good retrospective cringe, I recall standing in front of an audiences of boys and parents with a layout pad mounted on an easel, drawing puerile caricatures of well-known people – Mahatma Gandhi, Stanley Baldwin, Charlie Chaplin – at the same time spouting precocious-sounding patter that had been concocted for me by Mr Fox.

More importantly, Geoffrey Fox encouraged one of the younger masters who had an interest in jazz to form a band. Charlie Sheepshanks (who subsequently became headmaster himself) threw himself into moulding a 'jazz band' out of boys in some of whom a talent for music or any other form of juvenile showbiz had hitherto been unsuspected. Apart from the Swanee whistle, which he himself played with more infectious enthusiasm than finesse, the band consisted of kazoos and other toys that could be blown or hit – the latter in my instance, since I was the drummer (you must wait to learn how that came about). I have no doubt that the sound we produced on the concert platform was excruciating, but parents at school concerts are naturally inclined to be indulgent, and we had fun. It was then that I discovered the joy of making music in an ensemble, a crucial moment in any young musician's life.

A cluster of thoughts intrudes here. For the first, Chairman Humph has to give way to one of the greatest thinkers of them all.

A woman's preaching is like a dog's walking on its hinder legs. It is not done well; but you are surprised to find it done at all.

> Samuel Johnson, from Boswell's *Life of Johnson*, 1793
> (I append the date to ward off politically correct indignation)

Much the same might be said of both the Swanee whistle and the kazoo.

There is a certain symmetry in the fact that one of the most popular games in *I'm Sorry I Haven't A Clue* is called 'Swanee Kazoo' and calls upon the teams to perform brief duets on those instruments, the more excruciating the better. The Swanee whistle takes its name from the common corruption of Suwannee, a river in South-East Georgia, USA. The 'Swanee' river was brought to the world's attention by the American songwriter Stephen Foster, in his song 'Old Folks At Home', published circa 1870, better known to some as 'Way down upon the Swanee river' (I hope you're taking notes. This burst of erudition isn't going to last forever).

The instrument operates on the bicycle pump principle. I suppose the trombone is a better analogy, since it too relies on the player to alter the notes by means of a slide, without the assistance of keys or valves. Rhapsodising on the Swanee whistle is a hit-or-miss affair, more often used nowadays for comedy effect. (I don't know why I say nowadays – I'm sure the parents in the early thirties, listening with rapt expressions of pride to the Sunningdale jazz band sounding like a choir of drunken owls, were in fact suffering agonies of suppressed laughter.)

The onomatopoeically named kazoo is hardly more reliable, depending for its accuracy on the musical ear of the person who hums or sings into it. My reference books are reticent as to its origins. I guess that it was invented as a toy by some kindly person to replace the primitive comb and tissue paper combination, the tendency of which to make the lips itch must have nipped many a musical career in the bud.

PS: I should add in fairness that both instruments have had their place in jazz. The young Louis Armstrong played the Swanee whistle quite attractively on a couple of recordings by his Hot Five in the twenties (go to a piece called 'Who's It' for confirmation). Such was his innate genius that he could probably have done as well with a bicycle pump.

PPS: Later in that decade an ex-jockey and vocalist called Red McKenzie held his own in stellar company blowing through comb and paper (refer to 'One Hour' by the Mound City Blue Blowers, 1928), and the more hi-tech kazoo makes a number of appearances in the discographies.

PPPS: Followers of *I'm Sorry I Haven't A Clue* will have noticed the minor phenomenon that the satirical comedian Jeremy Hardy, who is unable to sing two consecutive notes in tune, can pitch perfectly when doing it through a kazoo.

*

It just occurred to me that I have never properly explained my association with 'the antidote to panel games', *I'm Sorry I Haven't A Clue*. I should have done so when the topic of silliness arose, since it has brought me to the peak of that desirable condition.

Towards the end of 1971, David Hatch, then wearing the twin hats of actor and BBC producer, rang me to say that the cast of a radio game-show called *I'm Sorry I'll Read That Again*, of which he was a member, were looking for a 'sister' show to fill in the periods when their show was off the air. Graeme Garden had come up with *I'm Sorry I Haven't A Clue*. Would I be the chairman in a pilot recording?

My experience of the few pilots that I had previously done led me to expect that I would be paid a studio fee to record a trial show which would then disappear without trace, never to reach the airwaves. So I agreed. With a team of Graeme, Tim Brooke-Taylor, Bill Oddie and Jo Kendall, we recorded a 'live' programme at London's Playhouse Theatre.

It was then totally improvised, not an easy thing to do in the short time allotted to a radio show. I can remember the panellists coming into the nearby Sherlock Holmes pub after the recording, still ashen after the ordeal. Someone asked David Hatch what chance there was of it ever being broadcast. His immediate answer was, 'None, except possibly after lunch on Boxing Day when the listeners are pissed.'

Nevertheless, he beavered away for the next month or two among the BBC planners, and eventually rang me to say that the show would start in February 1972. Barry Cryer and I shared the job of chairman for the first series. Then I took over when he joined Tim and Graeme in the regular team that, with the addition of Willie Rushton, became a fixture for many years. I am told that the person who has periodically set up an unholy din on the piano during much of that time is called Colin Sell.

What has come to be known as my 'feud' with Colin started when, on one show many years ago (it may have been last year, it just feels like many years ago), Barry Cryer addressed to me a query about one of the musical games and Colin rose from the piano stool and began to answer it, off-microphone, still wearing the headphones he needs to supplement his faulty hearing. It was a gross breach of elementary protocol and I was quite within my rights to cut him off with a peremptory, 'I'm the chairman, SIT DOWN!' Like many other things in the programme, it was allowed to develop into a regular part of the show, to the extent that Colin Sell's mother, so he told me, once said to him, 'Why do you allow that dreadful man to speak to you like that?'

If you suspect that Colin Sell and I are, in reality, good friends, I would ask you to keep it to yourself. We don't want ugly rumours like that to get around.

The freedom we have had, from a succession of producers, to allow small incidents to become running gags in the show sometimes has strange results.

Tim Brooke-Taylor and I sit alongside each other on stage. We are both connoisseurs of throat lozenges, often sharing when one or other of us has left his supply at home. During the preliminaries to one show, there was some consternation when we found that neither of us had brought any, relying on the other to have some at the ready. When the audience was in and the show was under way, Tim mentioned the dilemma more than once in the course of some ad-libbing. Suddenly, a single lozenge landed on the stage, thrown by a well-wisher in the circle. One of the team mentioned that the whole pack would have been more generous. Within seconds, the rest of the gold pack (we're talking Lockets here) came down in front of us. Had one of our regulars come to the theatre with pockets stuffed with assorted confectionery on the off-chance that one would be mentioned? This was one running gag that we hurriedly aborted. A Jumbo Toblerone or a bargain bag of Mars Bars could have inflicted serious injury.

I drove to the Playhouse that first time asking myself what, with an active day job, I thought I was doing, and how could I possibly do it among four top comic actors. The second question answered the first, and I have since clung to it to guide my on-air persona. I treasure as a compliment the reference to me in a newspaper review as 'the comatose chairman'.

It was a great blow when Willie Rushton died on 11 December 1996.

Up until then, the team had for many years been perfectly balanced. From my seat in the centre of a crescent-shaped set, perilously close to the predatory Samantha, I had plenty of time to assess the distinct role which each played: Barry, filling the gaps with a gag for every occasion and a miracle-worker's ability to bring back an old joke, alive and kicking, from the dead; Tim, the ever-so-slightly posh Englishman showing a hint of vulnerability that wins the sympathy of the audience (in early days, when I was in charge of the scoring, I was once booed and hissed for withholding points from him); Willie, lacing his gruff satire with irritability just below the surface; and Graeme, content to sit for minutes, inscrutable, until delivering a knockout punchline that will bring a round to an abrupt end. It was a wise decision not to try and replace Willie. Since then we have had a roster of talented and hilarious guests who have, in their own ways, kept us afloat.

When Willie died, it was uplifting and extraordinary to witness the love in which he was held throughout the country. At his funeral, we all had the same story, of strangers crossing the street to sympathise over our loss. I say extraordinary because he was not a man who courted easy popularity. It's not that he didn't suffer fools gladly. He didn't suffer them at all. Two anecdotes will suffice, second-hand but, I hope, accurately presented.

Those who believe that after-dinner speaking is simply a matter of rising to one's feet and spouting for twenty minutes or so have it badly wrong. Speakers are usually required to attend the lengthy dinner itself, sitting at the top table with the chairman and his guests and, while eating, joining in the conversation among complete strangers. When the host is hospitable and the company is congenial, it can be enjoyable, though rendering the brain numb by the time the call to stand up and scintillate arrives.

Willie Rushton once sat through a meal next to a chairman who made no effort to entertain or even speak to him. With corporate shop talk buzzing relentlessly around and across him, he became increasingly bored and irritable, until the moment came for him to make his speech. Then the chairman committed the ultimate breach of etiquette by ending his cursory introduction with the words, 'And I hope he's going to be funny because we're paying him a large amount of money tonight.' As he rose from his chair, Willie roared into the microphone, '. . . most of which is for sitting next to you for an hour and a half!'

I must preface the next entry by saying in advance that the object of one of Willie's most scathing put-downs received it with appreciative laughter.

In the years just before his death, Willie Rushton partnered Barry Cryer in a two-man show called *Two Old Farts*, with Colin

Sell at the piano. It was Colin who told me this story while we were assembling for Willie's funeral at the Mortlake Crematorium.

On tour, Willie and Barry arrived at a theatre early in order to rehearse for their evening performance which, being topical, required special preparation. They found a blind piano tuner already tuning the piano. They waited till he'd finished, then went onstage themselves to begin work. Instead of packing up and leaving, the tuner hung about, every now and then chipping in on their rehearsal with suggestions or comments. The interruptions were enough to light Willie Rushton's fuse and he became more and more restive, eventually stumping off the stage and heading for the sanctuary of the dressing room, normally a safe haven. But after a minute or two, the man appeared in the doorway, like some persistent spectre, this time rapping on about the virtues of the Guide Dogs for the Blind Association and the dog they'd trained for him. 'I'll let you see him if you like,' he piped and, despite the lack of enthusiasm which Willie was by now radiating in a malevolent aura, hurried off to fetch the animal, returning with a cry of 'Here he is!' Without turning from the table where he was working, Willie growled, 'How very cruel of them to give you a cat!'

*

I have a kazoo in the top drawer of my desk. The fact is, I have found it impossible through life to shed my childhood fascination for anything that will produce music, toy or otherwise. It's not just nostalgia. Every now and then, I reach for my kazoo and hum a few measures of a song into it. It has a curiously therapeutic effect, bringing balm to the soul (a phrase which I will explain later if you care to stick around). In the same drawer, there is a penny whistle. This is not the same one that my father once bought me (actually for a penny, so we're going back a bit). That was a present which my father didn't hand over until he had taught himself one tune, a Scottish ditty called 'Cock O' The North'. Though more successful on this than on the 'cello, he was definitely a one-tune man.

I suppose my subsequent curiosity about musical instruments places me in the category known clumsily in jazz jargon as a multi-instrumentalist. Today, the only instruments I play in public are the trumpet, the clarinet and, occasionally, the tenor horn (known in America perversely as an alto horn), though I have strummed a guitar inexpertly onstage in the distant past and can do a passable imitation of Count Basie for eight out of twelve bars of 'St Louis Blues'.

Having blown the trumpet and the clarinet during a session at the time-honoured jazz club at 100 Oxford Street (in the fifties, for almost a decade, the Humphrey Lyttelton Club, now called the 100 Club) I was accosted by a member of the audience who asked, in a not altogether friendly manner, 'Do you play more than one instrument to show off your virility?' It was a hot night and the place was crowded, so I just said 'Yes,' over my shoulder and ploughed on towards the band-room.

Had I had time and inclination to boast, I could have reeled off a list of instruments I have owned, withholding the fact that most, having been written off as failures or outgrown along the way, were either discarded or consigned to a remote cupboard. Before the trumpet became my ultimate destination, I became quite adept on the mouth organ, as we used to know the harmonica. Indeed, my first musical inspiration was Larry Adler, whose photograph was on my bedroom wall for a while. I graduated to the top-of-the-range Hohner model with the button at one end that achieves the semitones and enables the player to negotiate any required key. It came in what looked like a rosewood box, the feel of which I can still recall in a burst of nostalgia.

The blues singer and harmonica player Sonny Boy Williamson made several visits to Britain in the sixties. My former colleague of many years, pianist Stan Greig, accompanied him on various occasions. On the first of these, there was discussion at the bar beforehand as to what keys he favoured. 'Don't matter,' he said, 'I play all the keys, man, all the keys.' Most blues harmonica players use the fairly basic standard instrument in the one key, so Stan was impressed. Sonny Boy picked up and opened a large, flat wooden box with which he had arrived at the gig. Inside, neatly laid out in their own slots, were a dozen basic instruments of various sizes, one for each key. 'There you are,' he said. 'All the keys!'

The mouth organ is a vulnerable instrument, prone to blockage by a wide variety of detritus if stuffed carelessly into a schoolboy's pocket. I went through a number of replacements before Larry Adler came down off the bedroom wall to make way for Louis Armstrong, and my cherished Hohner De-Luxe was ousted by the trumpet.

It was some time later, and in different circumstances, that I met Larry Adler. He had come to live in London and for a while had a radio chat show on the BBC. When he interviewed me, I was then writing the restaurant column in *Harpers & Queen*, and in his introduction, he said that I had the most enviable job in the world, getting paid for eating. I remembered that, and when I left the magazine I recommended him as a replacement. He took over, but not for very long. I think perhaps it was a mistake, in the context of *haute cuisine*, to mention his vasectomy quite so often.

One of the thousand ways in which I fell short of Larry Adler was visually. To be frank, I didn't have the hands for it. In posed pictures of him in action, his fingers curled back expressively like those of an Indian dancer. In similar pose, I looked more like someone trying to eat a buttered corn-on-the-cob without getting stains on his tie. Most musicians will agree that, in their choice of an instrument in which to specialise, the visual element plays a part.

I was led to the trumpet not only by the sound made by my first idol, Nat Gonella, but also by the pictures which I saw in the music magazines of Louis Armstrong in heraldic posture, pointing the instrument skywards as if issuing a clarion call. I was not aware, until I began to attract some publicity myself, that this was almost certainly a photographer's notion. The crude fact that I learned was that, if that noble posture is adopted in practice, all the spit that accumulates in the instrument runs back into the mouthpiece, creating a 'bubbling' performance in a literal and unfortunate sense.

From the Chairman Humph 'Trumpet Tutor', as yet unwritten

For no reason than that it may come in useful later, here's a message by the jazz-loving Leonard Bernstein:

The gayest, wildest jazz always seems to have some hint of pain in it . . .

Leonard Bernstein, speaking of the jazz 'sound' in a recorded lecture entitled 'What is Jazz?'

I have discreetly kept to myself for many years the fact that when I had my tonsils out at a tender age, I was given a banjolele by my parents (more a small banjo than a ukelele) by way of compensation.

I was thrilled when I found it under the bed, but holding it and looking at it adoringly was one thing, learning it quite another, and it soon went. Quite honestly, it's not the sort of thing a chap wants to talk about.

Why is the banjo so unpopular? For some years now, it has been the object of ridicule among musicians, spawning an epidemic of ribald and derisory jokes. The Irish and mothers-in-law are nowadays relatively safe behind the protective screen of political correctness, but the banjo and its perpetrators are fair game and their persecution an open season.

Riddle: If you go into a room and see a good banjo player, a bad banjo player and a pink elephant, which one do you talk to?
Answer: The bad banjo player. The other two are figments of the imagination.

Example of a banjophobic joke

Banjophobia is not a contemporary phenomenon. In 1890, George Bernard Shaw was the music critic of a London newspaper, the *Star*, writing under the pseudonym Corno di Bassetto. His brief was a broad one, taking in light entertainment as well as classical concerts and recitals. On 14 March 1890, he reviewed a performance at the International Hall in London by two brothers advertised as 'the unique and incomparable Bohee Operatic Minstrels'. Shaw, like Winston Churchill, knew the rhetorical power of arcane phraseology to enhance mockery. It helps to read this with an Irish accent:

> The Bohee Brothers are themselves banjoists, and would have me believe that the Czar of Russia affects that weapon. Had I known this last Sunday, I should have made a much more vigorous speech in Hyde Park at the demonstration on behalf of the Siberian exiles. If it be true that the Prince of Wales banjoizes, then I protest against his succession to the throne. The further suggestion that Mr Gladstone favours the instrument is enough to bring that statesman down to the International Hall with his axe. The banjo may be as fashionable as the chimney-pot hat; but the Brothers Bohee could no more reconcile me to the one than Messrs Lincoln and Bennett to the other. The more featly they twanged the more evident they made it that no skill of handling could extenuate the enormities of the Ethiopian lute.

From the *Collected Works* of Corno di Bassetto

(Footnotes to the above: In this semantic minefield, a certain amount of translation is necessary. I have searched the dictionary in vain for 'banjoizing'. 'Featly' too, is elusive, but I'll give it the benefit of the doubt. Abraham Lincoln and Arnold Bennett customarily wore the chimney-pot hat, which looked like a tall and crumpled top hat that had seen better days. And Mr Gladstone, like George Washington, regularly chopped down trees as a respite from the affairs of State.)

As often happens when the unspeakable villain in a drama is finally humiliated, I begin, by the end of Shaw's assault, to feel sorry for the hapless Ethiopian lute (Shaw's phrase rolls off the tongue impressively but is inaccurate – the instrument originated in West Africa). Truth to say, I have little difficulty in turning devil's advocate on behalf of the instrument.

I once had a banjo in my own band. It was played by Freddy Legon, who also played guitar. One night, in a concert in Rouen, responding to wild calls for an encore from an overexcited French audience, I stamped my foot to beat in a reprise of 'Royal Garden Blues' and brought it down on the neck of Freddy's banjo, which he had unwisely laid on the floor. The blow reduced it to a Jackson Pollock abstract of splintered wood and tangled strings. At that time, I was on the cusp of a stylistic transition from traditional jazz to what had been dubbed 'mainstream'. The word was coined to describe a smoothly swinging style of music in which a banjo in the rhythm section is more a hindrance than a help. I am aware that it was, and perhaps still is, believed that the 'accident' was a drastic gesture, a break for freedom on my part. Not true, but it's a nice parable.

Much of the antipathy to the banjo in recent times derives from what is known as the Trad Boom, a brief period between 1959 and the arrival of the Beatles two years later. Recordings by traditional jazz bands crept into the pop charts, and in a very short time the landscape from Land's End to John O'Groats and across Europe teemed with 'Trad' bands, every one featuring a banjo in its rhythm section.

I imagine that the Bohee Brothers, who so disturbed Corno di Bassetto, were skilled banjo technicians using the fingerpicking style familiar in folk music. With some honourable exceptions, the Trad banjoists tend to be strummers. And since the harmonic structure of many of the tunes they play are basic, the strumming often lingers tediously on one chord. Played properly, the maligned instrument can sing with a sound that I choose to describe as 'plangent'. That's not only because, in its meaning of 'plaintive or sad', the word conforms to Leonard Bernstein's definition of the jazz voice as containing 'a hint of pain'. Applied to the banjo, it also sounds more than faintly onomatopoeic. So I say, 'Plang away regardless, you banjoizers!'

*

While I was at Sunningdale School I started having lessons at home on the military side drum. My father's brother Caryl Lyttelton, a vicar who did much work in the East End of London, gave me a battered old Boys' Brigade drum of the kind that is hitched on to a belt round the waist. As usual, I fell in love with it, to the extent that my mother, in search of a teacher, responded to an advert in the local paper. One evening Mr Glass, a former drum major in the Coldstream Guards, came to our house in Eton. My mother proudly explained that I had taught myself quite a lot on my Boys' Brigade drum, Mr Glass's answer was, 'Don't worry, madam – I'll soon unlearn him all that.' And he proceeded to do just that for several years.

Though there were many conventional hoops to go through before fulfilment, I am sure it was the combined influence of Sunningdale's headmaster Geoffrey Fox and Mr Glass at a formative age that laid the foundation of my ultimate career.

Ex-Drum Major Glass taught me many things and notably, how to read drum music. In later life, when I led a band that made much use of written music, I found myself finding it much easier to read the rhythmic patterns on sight than the notes which dance up and down on the page. Working then and now with musicians who are expert sight-readers, I have much the same feeling of guilt that I experienced when receiving awards as a restaurant critic in the fifties and sixties. I can however claim that once I have, with much labour in advance, mastered a piece of written music and performed it a few times, I can thereafter throw the manuscript away and remember it in perpetuity. That gives me the edge, I argue, over those who still have to scrabble for the band part when I call up an arrangement for the hundredth time.

I'm encouraged in this situation by another invaluable piece of advice given to me by Mr Glass.

As a member of a theatre orchestra in Windsor, he once invited me to sit with him in the orchestra pit for several performances of *The Mikado*, even handing me the sticks on the last night to play a brief roll on the drum to herald 'God Save The King'. When I expressed indignation, as children do, at having been exposed to such danger without warning, he said, 'Look, son – there was nothing I gave you to play then that you don't play a hundred times when you're practising at home.' He then added, pointing out into the auditorium from which the audience was making its shuffling exit, 'Never forget this. You've got the music in front of you, they haven't. If you make a mistake, just carry on as if you meant it. They'll never know.' I have been told that most concert soloists of international repute have, at one time or another, fallen back on that principle.

It was through Mr Glass's influence that my first great passion in music was for military marches. We lived two miles away from Windsor Castle and, more importantly to me, the Victoria Barracks down the road that housed in rotation the regiments of the Brigade of Guards. At half past ten in the morning, the band in residence would lead a march up to the castle for the changing of the guard. I was first taken to see this ritual by Mr Glass. Thenceforward through the short Easter holidays, I would be there every morning opposite the main gate of the barracks, holding my bicycle and waiting.

The parade would form up on the barrack square out of my vision but I could hear the barked words of command. To this day, I can without effort relive the charge of excitement triggered by the distant words, 'By the left . . . quick MARCH!' and the five-beat roll on the drums which announced that the band was at last on its way. It took thirty seconds or so for it to wheel into view at the gate, and for the excitement to become almost orgasmic as the brazen sound of a row of trombones hit me in the solar plexus.

It was through these excursions that I acquired another of my enduring heroes. The name of Kenneth Alford became known to me when I started buying gramophone records of the tunes to which I thrilled on those marches to Windsor Castle and back. (Mr Glass again introduced me to many of those tunes, not always reliably. Even as a nine-year-old I knew enough French to realise that '*Le Rêve Passe*' does not mean 'They shall not pass!') It was much later that I learned that 'Kenneth J Alford' was a pseudonym, concealing the true identity of Major Frederick Joseph Ricketts, long-time Director of Music for the Royal Marines.

His story turns out to be more romantic than that imposing name and rank suggests. He was born in 1881, the son of a coal-merchant in London's East End. Orphaned at the age of fourteen, he joined the army by faking his age, and was soon recognised as a musical prodigy. He was still a young man when, after training at the Army School of Music at Kneller Hall, he became bandmaster for the Argyll and Sutherland Highlanders and when subsequently he took up his post with the Royal Marines.

It was while Kenneth Alford was with the Argylls that he wrote his most famous march, 'Colonel Bogey'. From the moment the ink dried on his score, this masterpiece has been sorely traduced over the years. For a start its title is, for reasons on which we needn't dwell, liable to reduce small children to helpless giggles. The corners of my mouth twitched, I'm sure, when I first heard it from the mouth of Mr Glass.

Since then, of course, the tune has had to contend with not one, but two sets of bawdy lyrics that have been attached to it over the years by marching soldiers: 'Bollocks – and the same to you' offers little in the way of subtlety. But the other version, if not in the Johnny Mercer or Ira Gershwin class, shows signs of some poetic thought. I print it here as a tiny contribution to the sum of satirical verse, and for the benefit of those who, nowadays, look blank at any reference to it:

Hitler . . . has only got one ball,
Goering's . . . are very, very small,
Himmler . . . is somewhat simmler . . .
and as for Goebbels, he's noebbels at all.

Propaganda-wise, the ditty might well have helped us to win World War II. Alas, it has done little for 'Colonel Bogey'. The final indignity came with the adoption of Kenneth Alford's finely constructed piece as the theme for the David Lean film *Bridge On The River Kwai*. In providing the tune with what is known in the trade as a 'hook' in the form of the unison whistling of soldiers on the march, Matthew Arnold's adaptation did a good job. But in the process, it destroyed Kenneth Alford's own essential trademark.

Pause for a brief moment of trauma. I had already written the above words for the book when I watched an edition of the highbrow television quiz *University Challenge* in which the 'whistling' theme was played to the teams and they were asked to name the composer. I had shouted 'Kenneth Alford!' at the TV set (as one does in the privacy of one's living room) when I was aghast to hear Jeremy Paxman give to the flummoxed contestants the answer 'Malcolm Arnold'.

As a composer of military marches, Kenneth Alford is on a par with the great American, John Philip Sousa. They have much in common, notably the understanding that the primary purpose of a military march is to impart a feeling of pride, confidence and euphoria in those marching behind. It's the drill sergeant's injunction, 'Heads up . . . chests out . . . shoulders back!' set to music. But there is a not-so-subtle difference between the two of them. As one might expect, the American had the edge when it came to pizzazz – the flamboyance epitomised by 'The Star-Spangled Banner' with its sparkling piccolos, cavorting sousaphones and crashing cymbals. I've always thought of, and admired, Sousa's marches as concert rather than functional music. For one thing, the US Army marches differently from the British, in short (dare I say, rather prissy) steps that demand a brisk tempo. By contrast, the British Army has a measured tread that invites a more laid-back and, in jazz parlance, swinging tempo. You can't hurry 'Colonel Bogey'.

The quality that distinguishes Kenneth Alford's music more than any other is his use of countermelody, as rich and subtle as that of Duke Ellington in another idiom. In its original un-butchered form, 'Colonel Bogey' offers a supreme example. What goes on behind the familiar opening themes is significant and worthy of attention. But it's with the arrival of the third theme that a thrilling reversal takes places. Beneath the staccato *diddle-diddle-dum* semi-quavers by which the tune is usually identified, a sweeping melody unfolds.

Played by the band's middle-range instruments, the melody has a logical beauty that relegates the overhead stuttering of the cornets and clarinets to the status of what, in jazz, is called a riff. Removed from its context and played with feeling by a choir of 'cellos, it could take its place among the most noble motifs of orchestral music. To replace any part of Colonel Bogey with whistling, for whatever reason, can only be described as vandalism.

PS: Several theories exist as to the origin of the tune's title. I take this to be the official one. When in the Argyll and Sutherland Highlanders, Alford used to play golf with the colonel of the regiment, an indifferent player who, instead of shouting 'Fore!' when an erratic shot was heading for the cranium of some unheeding bystander, whistled two piercing notes of alarm. Alford used those notes to launch his tune. 'Colonel Bogey' was a sly reference to his senior's inability to score par on the golf course.

PPS: The origin of the 'Colonel Bogey' melody may have a parallel in so-called popular music. Larry Adler always said that

George Gershwin wrote his song 'The Man I Love' in response to a challenge, from another member of the Algonquin circle, to base a tune on the three notes usually applied by musicians, tongue-in-cheek, to the words 'Good evening, friends!'

Let's linger awhile on this subject of musical heroes. The names of Louis Armstrong and Duke Ellington have constantly recurred in this bumblebee excursion through my mind. Regarding the latter, here's another thought, prompted by one of the Duke's most magisterial pronouncements:

> I have never understood why this thing that people call jazz should take precedence over me!

This was Duke Ellington's somewhat aggrieved response (eavesdropped by me when he was giving an interview to students from the London School of Economics) to criticism in the musical press that his London concerts in 1958 did not contain enough jazz. He had more to say:

> When Louis Armstrong plays 'Pennies From Heaven' or Coleman Hawkins plays 'Body And Soul', they call it jazz. But when Duke Ellington plays Ellington, they say it's not. I don't understand that.

It's not difficult for us to understand the Duke's frustration. Like Louis Armstrong, he was already established in his career as a musician when, as the twenties unfolded, the infant word 'jazz' made its first unsteady steps into common currency. It's an irony that would not have been lost on Ellington that when the word became what would now be called a style icon in the mid-twenties, his name and his music were a fundamental part of the culture that defined the Jazz Age.

Too much talk stinks up the place.

Duke Ellington, *passim*

The talking started in earnest towards the end of the twenties when a body of people recognisable as jazz critics appeared on the scene in both America and Europe. In order for them to pass judgement on the music, they had first to define it. Rules, yardsticks, criteria, whatever you like to call them, were established in order to answer the question 'What is jazz?' By the time Duke gave his interview to the students in London and, indeed beyond that up to the present day, no one has ever come up with a plausible answer. But the rules remain, constantly amended and updated.

The Cotton Club, where Duke Ellington and his orchestra presided, was at the hub of Harlem's entertainment scene in the middle-to-late twenties. The air around it was redolent with the spirit of jazz. Yet many of the performers who contributed to it – Florence Mills, Ethel Waters, Bill 'Bojangles' Robinson, Adelaide Hall and many more – would not, by today's criteria, be acknowledged as jazz artists at all. We seem to have got ourselves in a bit of a pickle, as Nanny Viggers used to say.

I suppose we have to accept that continuous sniping from one quarter or another is the price of distinction in the arts. Happily, history has a knack of correcting the most eccentric of critical judgements, establishing a consensus that is more or less consistent. For example, it's now widely acknowledged that the arrival of the young double bassist Jimmy Blanton in the Ellingtonian ranks brought about a golden era in the orchestra's music in the early forties. At the same time it placed Blanton, in the space of little more than two years in a tragically short life, high among those players who have revolutionised their instrument's role in the music.

One of the most influential critics of the day, Dave Dexter Jnr, writing in the prestigious music magazine, *Downbeat*, earned for himself a less enviable place in jazz history. He homed in especially on some piano and bass duets that Blanton recorded with his leader and which brought his nimble, buoyant playing into sharp focus.

Quite possibly the most sickening, unmusical and thoroughly disgusting sides the Duke has ever needled (sic) are 'Body And Soul' and 'Mr J B Blues', which are nothing more than duets by the leader and Jimmy Blanton. The first title, a jazz classic revered by anyone who has ever sat in on a session, is hacked, slashed and brutally butchered by Blanton's bullish bass bowings. The blues is easily as frightful with Jimmy thumping his strings as well as sawing them. All standards for intonation are forsaken . . . a menu of bass–piano duets such as those mentioned above might well prove disastrous to Ellington's legion of fans, this scribbler included. Maybe it was a gag.

Dave Dexter Jnr in *Downbeat*, 1 June 1941

I needn't say much more about this, other than to invite the reader to go over it again, assuming Rowan Atkinson's slack-cheeked enunciation when it comes to the fever of alliterative consonants halfway through.

To this day, arguments have raged and billions of words have been expended in the bibliography of jazz on the subject of Duke Ellington's compositions. Claims have been made, some by disgruntled band members themselves, that many of Duke's most famous themes were in fact contributed by them to his repertoire. Some of these are acknowledged in composer credits – clarinettist Barney Bigard appears as co-writer of 'Mood Indigo', and trumpeters Bubber Miley and Cootie Williams on 'East St Louis Toodle-oo' and 'Echoes of Harlem' respectively.

I have no urge to jump into the argument at the deep end so late in the day. But in order to express a thought, let's just take a more obvious example of apparent plagiarism. Duke Ellington's 'Creole Love Call', vintage 1927, is built on themes recorded four years earlier by King Oliver's Creole Jazz Band under the title of 'Camp Meeting Blues'. Put side by side, Oliver's blues is totally forgettable while Ellington's 'Creole Love Call' is a classic. Do we rule the latter out of court on a technicality?

Always ready to help, I'll fish two quotations from the cloudy waters of memory. It is not contested that Duke Ellington arranged or orchestrated the borrowed motifs, developing them into memorable compositions. So it's reasonable to apply the familiar fragment of dialogue that originated in a *Punch* cartoon from the thirties, possibly by the great Frank Reynolds. I quote from memory.

> A vicar addresses an elderly parishioner who is tending his garden.
>
> 'You and the Almighty have made a wonderful job of this garden, George.'
>
> George, grumpily: 'You should 'ave seen it when the Almighty 'ad it to 'isself.'

The French essayist Michel de Montaigne said much the same thing, applicable to composer and writer alike, though they weren't quite so concise in the sixteenth century.

> The bees plunder the flowers here and there but afterwards they make honey, which is all theirs; it is no longer thyme or marjoram. Even so with the pieces borrowed from others; he will transform and blend them to make a work that is all his own, to wit, his judgement.

Bee or gardener, Duke Ellington's work was all his.

*

The commonest question that any aspiring jazz musician must be prepared to face is, 'Do you make it up as you go along?' The answer is, 'Yes, but we in the trade prefer to call it improvisation.' (Or rather, that's how it started. But always on the lookout for a juicy paradox, I note that the more complex the music has become, the more do eminent commentators resort to baby talk to describe it. I suppose it all started back in the forties when Charlie Parker and Dizzy Gillespie hoisted jazz on to a higher intellectual level – and called it bebop. Nowadays, to be cool, you have to take the dummy out of your mouth and say 'improv'. But not here.)

Nothing has brought more confusion to the understanding of jazz than the belief, enshrined in dictionary definitions, that it is founded on improvisation. The word has hung about since the music began, begging to be clearly explained. In its strict sense, that of 'spontaneous invention', it never had a free reign in early jazz. The musicians in a classic New Orleans band each had a specific role to play – the trumpet to define the theme, the trombone to provide the bass harmonies, the clarinet, freest of them all, to weave a decorative countermelody. The layman's question arises from the perception that, in New Orleans-style bands – and for that matter, informal jam sessions – no one is seen to be reading from written music.

The musicians are guided by the harmonic, melodic and rhythmic shape of the tune, by the conventional role they have to play and by the memory of the way they played the tune the night before, and the years before that. In this way, if their ears are in good working order, chaos is avoided. It may be improvisation of a sort, but free it is not.

'Freedom' is an iconic word in the story of jazz development. As applied to what, as long ago as the sixties, was labelled avant-garde, it meant escape from the restrictions of preordained melody, harmony, metre and tempo, all things which had guided jazz performance from New Orleans to the so-called New Age. (Watch out, another paradox coming.) The more jazz has fled from these 'restrictions', the more verbiage has been expended in critical efforts to pin it down. As I write these words, I can see on my shelf across the room a book entitled *The Freedom Principle: Jazz After 1958* by John Litweiler, which is at least an inch-and-a-half wide. I'm sure, were I to blow away the dust and open it, it would contain a wealth of profound thought.

But I'm doing my best here not to pontificate. As the word implies, that is the role of the Pontiff, and jazz has had its fill of popes laying down the law and, in some instances, talking an awful lot of papal bull in the process. It's best, perhaps, if I tell you a story . . .

In the sixties, I compèred a BBC radio programme called *Jazz Club*, which had been running for two decades and was by then recorded in advance – fortunately, as it turned out. Its then producer, Bryant Marriott, a musician himself, showed an admirable willingness to give exposure to all kinds of jazz, avant-garde not excluded. He booked, at regular intervals, a group called the Spontaneous Music Ensemble. It was led by drummer John Stevens and its members included trumpeter Kenny Wheeler, saxophonist Trevor Watts and trombonist Paul Rutherford, all musicians of great distinction. John himself died in 1994, after achieving respect not only in the field of experimental jazz, but also as a tireless worker in jazz education and encouragement at the community level.

So there is no mockery involved in my story. Indeed it shows the serious efforts the group made to explore the frontiers of jazz innovation. As presenter, I introduced four of their broadcasts, speaking to John Stevens before each one so that I could convey to the studio audience and the radio listeners beyond, some notion of how the group worked. On the first occasion, he told me that their *modus operandi* was to establish a theme, be it a few bars or even a few notes of written music, and to advance from it in whatever direction their collective and spontaneous ideas might take them. This seemed to me a logical extension of the method employed by jazz musicians through the ages in their search for individual freedom of expression.

But the logic didn't end there – in the band's next appearance a few months later, John was eager to explain that they had moved on. This time, there would be no theme, since its very existence as a starting point imposed a restriction. They would simply start to play, one musician taking a lead and the rest following in what might be described, in literal terms, as a free-for-all, though I was careful not to use that term in my introduction to the programme in case it should be interpreted as mockery.

Had we now reached the end of the road in the quest for freedom? The third broadcast by the group took a further step that, with the wisdom of hindsight, the alert reader of this narrative might already have anticipated. As John explained in our pre-broadcast chat, it had been decided that for one musician to start to play before the others implied an element of dictatorship which subverted the idea of total freedom.

What followed on the actual recording was the epitome of *reductio ad absurdum*. Bryant Marriott's voice called over the intercom, 'OK, stand by!' The red light came on and I made my brief introduction to launch the broadcast, ending with, 'Here they are, the Spontaneous Music Ensemble!' Nothing happened. The musicians stood onstage, their eyes rolling, their breath held, waiting for the spontaneous moment when they would all start to play simultaneously. After a few long moments of dead silence, Bryant came out of the recording booth to ask in some desperation, 'Do you think you could actually start to play?'

Well, eventually they did, but not before I had formulated the thought that, if this was freedom, give me 32 bars of 'Won't You Come Home, Bill Bailey' any day. It was an unworthy thought. I should have trusted a musician of John's palpable honesty to reach something of the same conclusion. For, sure enough, by the group's fourth broadcast, they had retraced their steps, with no apparent loss of exploratory zeal.

A postscript to this thought is provided articulately – as one would expect from the son of a distinguished novelist – by pianist and composer Nick Weldon, in an autobiographical note to one of his recordings:

There is a paradox in jazz and it is this. The more we strive to be individual voices, improvising freely in our advanced harmonic and rhythmic language, somehow the less individual we sound, and the less freedom we seem to have. If all the emphasis is on us as individuals and on the way we deploy the elements of improvisation, then all we achieve is the freedom to sound like ourselves all the time. The freedom to sound exactly the same in every tune.

In searching so strenuously for our freedom, our own prison do we make . . . Yet in the days before jazz harmony was written about, when Ben Webster could be content simply to play the tune, barely embellished, and to concentrate on improvising a mood for the song, somehow players achieved more individuality. Another jazz paradox, this, and the converse of the first, is the individual voice should be given to the player who does not demand it . . .

A further thought occurs. In his reference to the tenor saxist Ben Webster, a pillar of pre-modern jazz, Nick Weldon touches upon the element, common to every other form of creative art, that we can only call 'magic'. Today's jazz criticism seems to demand, ludicrously to my mind, that with every performance a musician should surprise by breaking the mould, being at the cutting edge or extending the idiom, to borrow some fashionable clichés. I would be happier if critics in general would switch off the analytical mind and give the music a chance to weave its spell. Perhaps they would give some evidence in the process that, like the rest of us, they are sometimes just carried away.

I don't deny that one of jazz music's most distinctive assets is its ability to surprise. That most perceptive of jazz commentators, the American writer Whitney Balliett, entitled one of his volumes of collected articles *The Sound of Surprise*. But there's yet another paradox here, if you can stand it. It's to be found lurking in the fact that most of Mr Balliett's articles were focussed not on 'live' performance but on recordings by the great jazz performers.

> If it was not for the historical fact that the birth of jazz coincided with the invention of the gramophone or phonograph, jazz would never have taken root in the cultural soil of America and, subsequently, the rest of the world.

> Chairman Humph in disgruntled mode. He hasn't got a word in edgeways for several pages

Given that, for most enthusiasts, jazz exists mainly in their record collections, what price the sound of surprise? There may be surprise, even shock, when we first put a recording of Louis Armstrong's 'West End Blues' or Charlie Parker's 'Ornithology' on the turntable or the CD tray. Thenceforward, with every play, we know what's coming. The surprise is gone. Yet, decades later, the recordings remain timeless masterpieces. What's more, they were recorded by musicians whose express purpose at the time was far from that of making musical history. Let's turn for the last word on the subject to Charlie Parker, the principle architect of Modern Jazz:

> It's just music. It's playing clean and looking for the pretty notes.

> Charlie Parker, from an interview in *Downbeat*, 9 September 1949

*

At this point, a quotation from my father occurs, prompted by that word 'magic' a while back.

> When Pamela was teaching Humphrey divinity, and was emphasising the incredible goodness of Christ, H, finding the wings of his imagination tiring in the void, asked, 'Was

he as good as Father?' When P, as is supposed, answered that he was even better, H gave up and has been an agnostic ever since.

From a letter from George Lyttelton to Rupert Hart-Davis
(*The Lyttelton–Hart-Davis Letters* published by John Murray)

This is not strictly true. From childhood days, and through Sunningdale preparatory school and Eton, I look back on a long period of religious acceptance. After all, indoctrination continued from mother's knee to quite thorough instruction at Sunningdale and thence on to Eton where it intensified in the run-up to confirmation.

After confirmation, I was authorised to attend Holy Communion every Sunday in the Eton Upper Chapel. I recall coming away from it with a distinctly holy feeling. I believe now that it was chiefly light-headedness inspired less by the ceremony itself than by the effect of an unaccustomed sip of red wine before breakfast. My experience of alcohol had, up till then, been confined to an investigative slurp of my father's whisky and soda in much earlier childhood. It was shared with my elder sister when we found his glass unattended on a sideboard. Finding that it tasted like cat sick, we concluded that my father was either ill and in need of strong and repulsive medication, or quite insane. Either way, it was worrying for a while.

PS: I still think that the combination of whisky and soda tastes like cat sick.

After I left school, belief gradually declined, lapsing into agnosticism and finally converting to atheism in a moment of conviction, which struck me with great clarity, and no obvious trigger, as I was driving homeward one morning past Luton on the M1. I mention that detail to establish that 'revelation' works both ways.

My mother's belief was absolute. At some time during the elongated period when I began to emerge from what I can best describe as benign brainwashing, I remember assailing her with sceptical views that I expected to develop into an argument. She stopped it in its tracks by saying, 'I don't want to hear anything about that because, if it's true, everything in life is meaningless.' My father, on the other hand, though firmly wedded to the principles – and the literature – of Christianity, quite often allowed glimmers of agnosticism to show.

This is the moment to introduce into the kaleidoscope Ludovic Kennedy (now rightly Sir Ludovic), a friend of Eton days who played the drums in my first schoolboy band and whose company (since we share memories and, I believe, a similar sense of humour), I have enjoyed enormously in sporadic moments since. He recounts a similar dialogue with his mother, though more detailed and at an earlier age:

> Was God watching us pray? I asked my mother. She hesitated before replying but then said yes, she was sure he was. All of us, I asked, and all of us at the same time, and the people at the other church in the village as well? Yes, my mother said, but not all that convincingly. How did he manage that, I said, did he have a thousand pairs of eyes and ears? Ah, said my mother, that was one of the wonderful things about God, he could do things that human beings couldn't do.
>
> Ludovic Kennedy, *All In The Mind – A Farewell To God*
> (published by Hodder and Stoughton, 1999)

When Ludovic's closely argued and scrupulously researched book was published, it was interesting that it caused so little reaction. On our last meeting, on the occasion of my eightieth-birthday concert at Edinburgh in 2001, I wanted to ask him if he didn't feel some disappointment at not having been burned at the stake. When it came to it, the opportunity didn't arise. I suspect the answer would have been 'Yes', but given with that mischievous twinkle in the eye that looks out from his book's dust cover.

No one can have lived through the jazz experience over the decades without the realisation that human beings find it difficult to absorb unfamiliar ideas unless they are clearly labelled. Classic, Modern, Mainstream, Bebop, Post Bop, Free Form – these are just a handful of the ludicrous sign-posts that have served over the years to divert people from an understanding of a music that is indefinable. The same applies to religion. The notion of a supreme Someone who loves and protects us all individually and to whom, though we have no idea what or where he is, we can speak and, indeed, apply for an instant remedy to our problems is as unbelievable to me as it was to the young Ludovic. Nor do I think it sensible to prepare children for a long life on this planet by teaching them to reiterate constantly, through prayer, that they are unworthy sinners who must forever beg forgiveness. If that puts me in the Humanist pigeonhole, so be it. It's a label that, as Ludovic Kennedy goes to some lengths to affirm, does not rule out the concept of spirituality.

*

The dichotomy in my parents' religious approach became especially apparent when, between 1929 and the outbreak of war a decade later, we went regularly to Harlech in North Wales for the long summer holiday. Every Sunday, my mother would take us to church. And every Sunday she would say, 'George, you are coming with us, aren't you?' Ever ready with an apt and useful literary quotation, my father's answer would always be the same. 'No. I shall be worshipping in the vast cathedral of immensity.' He was referring specifically, as we children soon discovered, to the St David's golf course.

Writing these words, it occurs to me that there is a link between my father's adherence to Christianity and, while it lasted, to my own. His great passion was for literature, as will be apparent to anyone who has read not only his long correspondence with Rupert Hart-Davis, but also the publication of his Commonplace

Book *(George Lyttelton's Commonplace Book,* published by Stone Trough Books, 2002). My 'great passion', if I may repeat the lofty phrase, is for music, to which I have, for as long as I remember, been as susceptible as he was to poetry, which could on occasion reduce him to tears.

As a small child, I could hardly bear to listen to the tragic cadences of 'Who Killed Cock Robin?', and when the song came to the bit where all the birds in the air fell a-sighing and a-sobbing, I was right there with them. I recall this very clearly because, though so many years have gone by since then, the recollection of those poignant words and, more importantly, the musical cadence which carries them, still gives me a frisson of unaccountable sadness.

In this context, I have another popular misquotation to hand. Noel Coward had one of his characters in the play *Private Lives* famously comment on 'the potency of cheap music', and the quotation has often been attributed to the playwright himself. It's a phrase which has the sort of ring that a famous quotation should have if it is to carry through the ages. In fact, the words he actually used were unrhythmical, flabby and of dubious grammar:

It's extraordinary how potent cheap music is.

Noel Coward

To an unqualified admirer of Noel Coward's genius for felicitous – and fastidious – phrase-making, the quotation is disappointing. But where I question it is in the use of the word 'cheap', presumably in its dictionary definition as 'easy to get, more showy than sound, of little account'. Music is music, and its power to move has nothing to do with class or economics.

The late Robin Ray once presented a BBC radio series called *The Tingle Factor.* In it, weekly guests, more or less well known, chose musical items which gave them the little charge of electricity that sends a shiver down the spine and calls the hairs on the back of the neck to attention. My selection, including as it did Louis Armstrong's 1939 recording of 'Struttin' With Some Barbecue' and Kenneth Alford's march 'The Standard of St George', clearly left the spine and back hairs of my distinguished host unmoved but caused his eyebrows some agitation.

When it came to what is commonly known as Handel's Largo, sung on record by the greatest tenor of them all, Beniamino Gigli (all right, discuss), I began to propound my theory that certain musical cadences have a strange power to move the listener, citing in evidence the notes that accompany 'all the birds in the air' from 'Who Killed Cock Robin?' It also occurs in the climactic moments of the Largo, the lower harmony part of 'Abide With Me' and Billy Fury's sixties hit 'Stairway to Paradise'. (I'm goose-pimpling all over as I recite them). In the face of a blank look and a hurried change of subject from Robin Ray across the studio table, my cherished theory foundered and a valuable item of profound musicology failed to reach the public domain.

I became aware then of the truth that one man's Tingle Factor is another man's 'What's It All About, Alfie?' and that a roomful of small children exposed to 'Who Killed Cock Robin?' would not inevitably lead to an orgy of mass blubbing. I speak for myself alone when I say that, if I look back at moments when I have experienced what I might once have described as a surge of religious fervour, I find that music has almost invariably been responsible. Hymn singing at Eton College was far removed from what has been described as the 'Anglican drone' familiar in poorly attended parish churches. In the senior or 'Upper' chapel, it involved five hundred or more boys whose voices had matured from the croak of impending puberty to full-throated bellowing, and it was not difficult to become inspired with something or other in the midst of that.

In recent times, I have been to carol services in the Albert Hall at Christmas solely to enjoy the freedom, in the security of numbers, to bellow the harmonies of 'Hark, The Herald Angels

Sing' to my heart's content, while harbouring intact the knowledge that if at any time a Herald Angel were to come knocking on my door I would firmly but, I hope courteously, request him, her or perhaps it, to move on.

It's another memory that comes knocking on my door at this very moment. Unfortunately, it's too threadbare to fill a chapter of its own headed: MY PART IN THE FUNERAL OF KING GEORGE V.

But there, it's got its title nonetheless.

King George V's funeral took place at St George's Chapel in Windsor Castle in 1936. At Eton College, we had an Officers' Training Corps, an institution shared, I believe, by most public schools. Through it we periodically had the opportunity to dress up in khaki and play soldiers. A contingent from the Eton OTC of which I was a member was invited, or more likely commanded, to line part of the route to the chapel.

As the cortège slow-marched by, I recall feeling a sizeable lump in the throat. Why? George V was, to a schoolboy, a remote figure, all the more so since his voice, heard on rare broadcasts to the nation, carried guttural traces of his Saxe-Coburg descent. I'm unlikely to have been overcome with sorrow on behalf of Queen Mary, though I did actually clap eyes on her once in Windsor High Street when she stepped out of a Rolls-Royce almost into my path and disappeared into a shop amid a flurry of equerries. Once memorably described by Nancy Banks-Smith in the *Guardian* as looking always as if she were revolving slowly while people threw jewellery at her, Queen Mary gave me the impression, in her outdoor clothes, so to speak, of an impenetrably stern figure that had been stuffed into creaseless rigidity by an over-zealous taxidermist.

So, no cause for a trembling lip there. As for the royal princes, in step and expressionless behind the coffin in their assorted military attire, I remember them as no more than animated cardboard cut-outs – with the exception, perhaps, of Edward,

Prince of Wales, whose lop-sided eyebrows, one higher than the other beneath a furrowed brow, made him look always as if he were about to burst into tears (which, given the glum turn his life took after the abdication, was probably the case).

I am aware, of course, that I have been fleshing-out a memory as grey and fuzzy as an old newsreel with impressions acquired from other sources. What I do know without doubt is that it was the music from the band of the Brigade of Guards, by then halted just beyond my sight, which got to me. They played a funeral march, the melody of which, albeit it in a major, rather than the customary minor key, has stayed with me ever since. It requires no more than four bars from the score of Handel's Dead March from *Saul*, if intoned slowly to myself in the right sombre tones and with an imaginary thump on the massed bass drums at the start of each bar, to activate that icy tingle.

Speaking of funerals, which we were, and the responses of young children to television, which we weren't, at the age of seven our second son David was watching Winston Churchill's funeral with us in 1965.

A sombre thought occurred to him and he asked, with some apprehension, 'Are people always killed when they reach 91?'

*

A totally unrelated story has just come into my mind. So, exorcising in one go some of my least favourite clichés of telephone-speak, bear with me while I run it past you. I'll get back to you on spiritual matters later.

Our first-born son, Stephen, is blessed with a resourceful wit that has seen him through some awkward situations. At the age of ten, he and a school friend amused themselves one afternoon outside our house (which is called Alyn Close) by hitting small pebbles from the gravel drive high into the air over Barnet Road with tennis rackets. Fortunately, the road was less busy than it is nowadays. Nevertheless it was inevitable that, sooner or later, one would fall on a passing car. A man, his face puce with rage, stormed up the drive. 'You!' he shouted, pointing at Stephen. 'Are you belting stones?' He was stopped in his tracks by Stephen's calm answer, 'No, Alyn Close.' I have since toyed, at times, with the idea of changing the name of our house to Belting Stones – it has an aristocratic ring.

On the other hand, I'm not fond of stately homes. I saw plenty of them in my youth, as almost every relative or friend whom I visited lived in one. On one early occasion I had the traumatic experience, for a schoolboy, of finding, when I went upstairs to change for dinner, that the suitcase which had been taken to the room by a member of the household staff on my arrival had been unpacked and its crumpled contents laid out on the bed or stowed away in drawers. I felt the same sense of violation that is expressed by burglary victims when they discover that an intruder has been rootling round among their belongings.

Clearly, I have never got over it. Sometimes while on tour, I am booked by a promoter into a five-star hotel that has stately-home pretensions. Uneasiness begins when I find myself driving up a long gravel drive flanked by rhododendrons. It turns to panic when, as I reach the portals, a man wearing a top hat, ankle-length coat and, even in mid-summer, gloves – all quite often in a mock-regal shade of pale blue – emerges, waving to waist-coated minions to attack me and seize every item of my belongings. It's not simply a Scrooge-like aversion to having to tip each one of them at every stage of the journey from reception to bedroom, though for a guest who discovers on the way up in the lift that he has no loose change other than five pence and a few coppers, that can be humiliating enough. Among other more serious indoctrinations to which my upbringing exposed me was the notion that, in life, there are a myriad things which are – to use a dreaded phrase (now, I'm glad to say, largely extinct) – 'not done'. By resolutely *doing* them throughout adult life, I have managed to banish them. However, there are still places in which they make a sneaky return, if given the chance – and five-star country-house hotels are among them. For one thing, in the atmosphere of hushed rectitude, nothing interesting ever happens. One has to move down the ratings a bit for that.

Years ago, I stayed with the band in a smallish hotel in Shropshire. After the concert we sat up in the lounge talking and drinking into the small hours. At 7 a.m. I was awoken by a thunderous banging on my door. When eventually I managed to grunt an audible response, a female voice called out cheerily, 'Be a sport, love, let's 'ave yer sheets.'

It is clearly the ambition of those who build and run five-star country hotels that they should attain the sort of style and comfort of the big stately homes of old. I have news for them, which can be conveyed in a few paragraphs.

My father was brought up in Hagley Hall, the family seat in Worcestershire. In 1917, he wrote about it in these terms to his friend, Charles Fisher, who was coming to stay for the first time.

> Hagley is a place which might appear to some to possess considerable drawbacks. The Black Country is close by and sends forth a blight over the land when the wind is in the north, and the rain often falls with pitiless concentration when the wind goes to the south . . . the house itself was built before comfort was much thought of, and has changed little. Unless you were in luck your general impression might be that there was no light, natural or artificial, that the bells didn't ring, nor the clocks go, nor the windows open, nor the taps run.

It's only fair to say that in recent times the house has been smartened up and, indeed, opened to the public. Among the historical exhibits in the hallway hangs the death warrant issued after my ancestor, Humphrey Lyttelton, had been hanged for his part in the Gunpowder Plot. A musician friend who played at a function there a year or two ago came back to tell me drily and rather unkindly, 'Hey, they've got one of your write-ups framed in the entrance!'

Though I went to Hagley often as a child, I have fewer sharp memories of it than I have of Babraham Hall in Cambridgeshire, the home of my maternal grandparents. I have written quite a bit here about its occupants. These are a few impressions of the Hall itself.

Babraham Hall now houses the Babraham Institute, an agricultural research establishment. It's an imposing, red-brick building, stately enough but not handsome. It looks, as someone said about the camel, as if it had been designed by a committee – though an outline of its history in the Institute's brochure would have us believe that the seemingly random medley of ornate extrusions, chimney stacks and non-functional turrets was designed in the Jacobean style by Philip Hardwicke in 1832 and took five painstaking years to complete.

The interior, when my grandparents were there, was spacious and gracious, pervaded by a subtle and evocative aroma that sometimes revisits me in a whiff of nostalgia. But I couldn't then, and I can't now, describe it or identify its origin. In the dining room, from the walls of which the mounted heads of once four-legged creatures, from a glum buffalo to dainty antelopes, stared down with varied expressions of indignation, one might detect the whiff of something less attractive.

In one corner, stood on its hind legs, was a more impressive testimony to my grandfather's prowess as a big-game hunter. It was a stuffed bear, standing I would guess about five-foot-six (I was about to write 'in its stockinged feet' but that would have been ridiculous. My grandfather would have run a mile from any bear wearing stockings). With arms raised and teeth bared, it was clearly intended to display snarling aggression. But the taxidermist hadn't got it quite right and, wearing what resembled a silly grin, the bear gave the impression of a very drunk undergraduate at a college ball trying to entice a reluctant girlfriend on to the dance floor to do the lambada. In the matter of bodily hygiene, stuffed animals have a problem, and from this one, a musty smell emanated of dried hair and decayed plaster. I know, because when no adults were around we used to sneak in and dance with it.

In describing a house of such elegance and fragrant memories it seems unfair to pick on a contrasting aspect, but I have to put the record straight. I called the curious, asymmetrically positioned turrets which sprout from the roof of Babraham Hall non-functional, but there was one notable exception.

One of the turrets, rising from the ground floor to high above the roof, housed at its base a loo – not the compact modern sort, but one that depended on gravity to fulfil its function. So the cistern was fixed to the wall high above the seat, from which altitude a purposeful tug on the long chain could release a cataract that did the trick. Looking upwards from the seat, the occupant had an uninterrupted view of the sky through the glass-domed roof of the turret high above. But in the hot summer months, that view was clouded by the mass invasion of flies. There would be hundreds of them, buzzing about in a frenzy of activity until, brief lifespan exhausted, they dropped to the floor feet upwards with a tiny blip that is the fly equivalent of a dull thud. The fact is that hygiene, of the meticulous sort that we pursue today, was not high on the agenda in stately homes. *Laissez-faire* ruled, and year by year nothing was done to control or banish the flies. I must say they never bothered me, minding their own business and leaving me to mine.

In this trilogy of stately homes, I suppose Longford Castle in Wiltshire was the odd one out, in that I can't recall any shortcomings where hygiene or comfort were concerned. The sixteenth-century building was founded, and has been inhabited ever since, by the Pleydell-Bouverie family into which my mother's sister Helena married. It's a splendid building and in contrast to Babraham, all swooping symmetry.

Like Babraham, it was the scene of great family gatherings at Christmas. Despite its age, there was nothing spooky about it, as I recall, during the daytime. But at night, the huge corridors that linked the bedrooms creaked loudly and ominously throughout the dark hours, as if sending sinister messages to each other. It didn't help that among the party games we played after dinner was Murders, a forerunner of the current *Cluedo*, which involved walking round alone in the dark waiting to be pounced on by a selected murderer or to stumble over a shrieking victim. Even at around twelve years old I wasn't too good in the dark and often lay awake listening to the muttering floorboards and waiting for sunrise and the reassuring dawn chorus.

One night when there were no games my cousin Anthony and I were in his bedroom quite late listening to a dramatisation of *Jane Eyre* on the radio. With the introduction of Grace Poole, the housekeeper believed to be responsible for maniacal noises in the night, we became uneasy and simultaneously decided to switch off. After we had chatted for a while, curiosity got the better of us and we switched on again, to hear nothing at first but heavy breathing and scratching. It was broken by the tremulous voice of Jane Eyre asking, 'Who's there?' More silence and then, suddenly, a ghastly chuckle. We didn't wait to discover that it wasn't Grace Poole at all but the deranged Mrs Rochester from upstairs. Our heads almost met as we both dived for the off-switch.

Back in my room, I lay in a cold sweat listening to floorboards whose every apprehensive creak seemed to herald the approach of the staring-eyed lunatic whom I took to be Grace Poole. Once or twice I distinctly heard a grotesque chuckle outside my door. Looking back on it now, I think it might have been a pigeon on the windowsill.

*

Where was I when I so rudely interrupted myself? Ah, spirituality. It's important to detach the word, and the concept, from religion. If that leaves me with a responsibility to define it, then I shall call on that most magical of singers, Peggy Lee, to provide me with a get-out clause.

Here's a song that doesn't need talkin' about, just singin'.

Peggy Lee, *passim*, introducing the Arthur Schwartz and
Dorothy Fields song, 'Make the Man Love Me'

I feel the same about the concept of spirituality, which is why I hand over once again to Ludovic Kennedy, who puts it better than I can.

The Church has always assumed that they alone are the guardians of the spiritual, and that a sense of the spiritual plays no part in the make up of non-believers. They are wrong . . . I have gained more spiritual refreshment from nature and from art than any other single source.

Ludovic Kennedy in his book *All In The Mind*

Making the perhaps unnecessary observation that 'nature' includes my fellow human beings, I think that says it all. I avoid gingerly the word 'transcendental' in all this. The fewer long words the better. After all, that's what Nanny Viggers meant, way back in those nursery days, when she would say, 'You're down in the dumps – you need to do something to take you out of yourself.'

Where Ludo speaks of spiritual refreshment, I favour the term that I've used earlier: 'balm to the soul' can be found anywhere.

It's so calming watching the Newtonian law of physics played out on the snooker table.

Stephen Fry in the *Independent*'s 'Quotes Of The Week',
7 May 2006

In the spirit of the rest of this hotchpotch, let's pursue that theme and see where it takes us.

A view of Mount Snowdon on approaching Harlech from Dolgellau on Sunday, 26 August 2001

Since Snowdon has been in that same place for thousands, if not millions of years, it may seem quirky to pick on that one particular date. But having spent ten family summer holidays in Harlech between 1929 and the outbreak of World War II, and returning several times to the area with my own family in the seventies, I know all too well the unreliability of that view. Seen from the south, Snowdon is indeed a noble mountain, rising in an almost perfect triangle save for a little tick-shaped indentation, like a mark of identification, on the western slope. Sometimes the whole triangle is veiled in mist, at others there will be a persistent cloud perching on top of the mountain like a barrister's wig, covering the peak. Even when the summer skies are clear blue, a heat haze lends greyness to the distant silhouette. What I saw on that day, driving to a gig in Harlech was, to me, unique.

The road northward from Barmouth to Harlech bends very gradually to the right around a shoulder of high hills. Thus the panorama of the Snowdon range to the north of Tremadoc Bay is revealed to the traveller peak by peak with the tantalising deliberation of a striptease. Driving us as children along that route, my father, who exercised fiscal prudence when it came to pocket money and the like, would offer a reward of a penny to the first one of us to spot Snowdon. Of course, we shouted optimistically as each elevation of the skyline appeared, rising to a unison shriek of short-lived triumph when Mount Hebog, the only serious pretender to the throne, hove in sight. Nearer to us than Snowdon, Hebog was certainly impressive, though its appearance – lumpish and with a plateau at the summit that looks as if it had been sheared off by some massive low-flying aircraft – serves only to emphasise the nobility of its neighbour.

I had a colleague with me in the car on that autumn day in 2001, and I played my father's game. But even I was overwhelmed by what we saw as we drove out of the village of Llandanwg and rounded the corner. It was a warm late afternoon and the sky was blue. In the light of approaching autumn, the outlines of Snowdon were sharply etched, and the colours, a subtle blend of purple, green and brown, clearly defined. For the first time ever, I was looking at perfection. Trumpeters in full heraldic regalia should have been there to play a fanfare. The green room in the Theatr Ardudwy where we played that evening has a balcony from which the magnificent view could be seen and I went back to it again and again, taking colleagues with me and enthusing until their eyes glazed over and the sun went down. I have used the word 'noble' more than once, and I know no better one for Snowdon. Over the years I have marvelled at the magical way in which, in the accident of geological evolution, Nature has endowed that lump of rock with a grandeur and, yes, nobility appropriate to the highest mountain in the principality of Wales. Never has Snowdon proclaimed so loudly and imperiously, 'Look at me – I am the King!' as on that August day five years ago.

OK, I've waxed lyrical, but that's the way balm to the soul works. And a bit of waxing is no more than it deserves. That's why I'm giving my recollections these portentous titles.

The brief moments involving Billie Holiday and Lester Young in The Sounds of Jazz, an American TV programme, vintage 1957

My copy of this video is old and scratchy, but a treasured possession. In the course of it, Billie Holiday, after a short spoken introduction in her then ravaged voice, starts to sing her song 'Billie's Blues', accompanied by a group of jazz giants. There comes a moment when Lester Young, who up till then had wafted around the studio in a haze of marijuana and/or alcohol, taking no part, suddenly rises from the bottom of the screen like a spectre from the sea to deliver one chorus of the blues. Both he and Billie were then only months away from death, and the energy of his early playing had ebbed to a vestigial point. Yet the simple melody that he played, culminating in a profoundly moving phrase in the seventh and eighth bars that droops disconsolately at the end, is one of sheer beauty.

In the course of it, the camera cuts to Billie Holiday on her stool a little way away. In their younger days, she and Lester Young had established a closeness that bordered on a love affair. Since then they had drifted apart. What was it that prompted him to join the accompanying band unexpectedly when she started to sing, the only time he showed any interest in taking part? And as she nodded or shook her head at every turn of his solo, was it in sadness and regret, as it appeared to be? We can't tell for certain. But to me it has always been deeply moving to watch and, if we admit the Greek principle of catharsis into the ingredients, balm to the soul.

I have a postscript to the above. It comes from Volume 9 of the theatre critic James Agate's monumental diary entitled *Ego* (published by Harrap). In a letter to *The Times* in 1945, Agate entered a discussion then rumbling on concerning England fast bowler Tom Richardson and his failure to break the Australian innings in the Manchester Test Match of 1896, which England lost by a few runs. First he quotes the legendary cricket writer, Neville Cardus, on Richardson's reaction when the match ended:

> He stood at the bowling crease, dazed. Could the match have been lost? Could it be that the gods had looked on and permitted so much painful striving to go by unrewarded? His body still shook from the violent emotion. He stood there like some fine animal baffled at the uselessness of great strength and effort in this world. A companion led him to the pavilion, and there he fell wearily to a seat.

Agate then quotes the booming response of another writer, H J Henley, to whom he had relayed Cardus's words.

I won't have it! After the winning hit, Tom legged it to the pavilion like a stag and got down two pints before anybody else.

Agate's letter then goes on to observe that Cardus admitted to him years later that he was not at the ground, being seven years old at the time. H J Henley was fourteen and could have been there. Agate himself was nineteen, and remembered it well.

> In the mind's eye, I can see two Australians and eleven Englishmen legging it to the pavilion with the tall figure of Tom Richardson leading by many yards.

The significance of my postscript is this (thanks for waiting). Agate concluded his letter with these words:

> If a historian should tell me that Napoleon remained rooted to the field of Waterloo hours after the battle was lost I should know that he was speaking essential truth; that he skedaddled as fast as post-horses could leg it is correctness of a lesser order. Cardus, who watched the great match at the age of seven behind the bars of his nursery window some miles away, had the secret of the higher truth. But on the lower ground he taradiddled.

Likewise, if an eye-witness should tell me that after 'Billie's Blues' had been recorded Billie Holiday legged it out of the studio without a backward glance, and that Lester admitted afterwards that he was so stoned he didn't know she was there, I would have to accept it as correctness, but of a lesser order. My account is the higher truth, and will continue to give balm to the soul whenever I watch it.

The trees in Barnet Road, North London EN5, after a wet winter

Recurring balm, this. On a trip to Italy with my band a few years ago, I became irritated when, on a bus ride across the hills, they rhapsodised about the wooded scenery, as if it were something one had to go abroad to experience. When it comes to trees, I am unashamedly nationalistic. Britain has the best trees in the world. Driving on motorways the length and breadth of the country, the variegated copses and woodlands are a constant joy. In autumn, the colours are nothing short of balm to the soul. (On the German autobahns, by contrast, travelling through those endless ever-so-green conifers feels like a trip through a giant toothbrush.)

Where I live, behind my own trees, on Barnet Road, the borough council has at some stage imposed a preservation order on all trees. I drive into Barnet to do my shopping with a corridor of magnificent foliage lining the road, as if I were a person of some importance. It's all I can do not to take my hand off the wheel to give that little upturned wave to left and right, like the Queen.

*

I've come to a diversion. In 2005, I was invited to a reception at Buckingham Palace to celebrate British music. Five hundred musicians were there, filling several rooms which were visited by members of the royal family. I was lucky to be in a group of rock musicians, jazz people and composers presented to the Queen, and to witness a rather endearing moment when she met some of the guitarists. The newspapers were eager to make something of her question 'What do you do?' addressed to Eric Clapton but, to his credit, he wouldn't play their game. When she moved on to Brian May, the ex-member of Queen, she was more circumspect. 'Do you play guitar too?' He answered, 'Yes, I played on your roof during your Golden Jubilee party.' Like someone for whom a rather disturbing mystery has been solved, she said, 'Oh, it was YOU!'

Who else would you want as a head of state? I was once presented to the presidential Lady Thatcher, and experienced the notorious Thatcher handshake that could, in one firm movement, simultaneously welcome you and propel you sideways in the direction of the exit. So I know where I stand on the matter.

Is it my imagination, or do all today's politicians look and sound alike? Don't worry, I'm not about to embark on an in-depth study of the trend towards uniformity at Westminster. This is just my excuse to put in my favourite story about one of the great, irreplaceable characters of the past.

George Brown, when Labour Foreign Secretary in Harold Wilson's government, went to Peru to represent Britain at a large international conference, taking with him a reputation (enviable or unenviable, according to your viewpoint) as a formidable drinker. This is my version.

At the end of the conference there was a banquet, held in a huge ballroom with a band in attendance. Along one side of the room was the top table, at which the statesmen sat and from which they made speeches in turn. Across the floor was an area occupied by Peruvian VIPs.

When the meal was over, George Brown spoke first, then sat down and went to sleep. He was woken an hour or so later by the band striking up. Looking around, he saw people beginning to stand up, and assumed that the formalities were at an end and dancing would begin. He got up, walked round the table, teetered across the ballroom floor and made for a stately vision of loveliness, dressed in red from head to foot, whom he had noticed earlier in the evening.

He said to the vision of loveliness, 'Dear lady, would you do me the honour of dancing this waltz with me?' The vision of loveliness looked down and answered, 'I will not dance with you for three reasons. The first is, you're drunk. The second is, this is not a waltz, it's our Peruvian national anthem. And the third is, I am not your "dear lady", I am the Cardinal Archbishop of Lima!'

*

If one stubbornly persists in blowing a trumpet at the age of 85, one must expect questions on the lines of 'How on earth do you keep going?' or sometimes, a more matey 'Where do you get your puff from?' I shall address them later. But first I must cite, as some sort of an inspiration, the example of Jack Jenkins. Some time after we had our house built in Arkley, Hertfordshire in 1959, he came to do our garden once a week, having recently retired from Laing's, the construction firm. When I say 'do the garden', I don't just mean the hoeing and mowing.

One Friday I went out to tell him I was planning to make a fish pond on the grass at the back. (You had to go outside to discuss these things, he was a shy man who would never come inside the house, even to drink a cup of tea.) My wife Jill and I were out all day visiting the RSPB headquarters at Sandy. We returned to find that, in our absence, he had dug a hole in the lawn large enough to trap an elephant.

It was not unusual to look out on a Friday and see him – tall, wiry, apple-cheeked, with his weathered cap a fixture on the small head – carrying unaided great boulders of York stone or bags of compost from one end of the garden to the other. In all the years he was with us, he gave no indication that he would like us to call him Jack – it was always Mr Jenkins or, when speaking of him in his absence, Jenks. In the later years, when we guessed that he was in his seventies, I was reluctant to ask him to take on heavy jobs. I had learned from experience that the way to get him to volunteer – to chop down a tree, perhaps, or move a summer-house – was to say that I intended to hire a firm to undertake the work. His answer was always the same: 'Oooh, you don't want to do that – I'll 'ave it done next Friday.'

In 1987, the now historic hurricane flattened a quince tree that Jill had planted many years earlier. It had reached a height of about twenty feet, had for some time fruited quite prolifically and was now lying flat on the grass. We never quite got around to chopping it up, so it lay there till spring when, surprisingly, we spotted leaves sprouting. It was still alive. Quince trees have shallow roots that spread outwards below the grass. The collapse had dragged them to the surface, but they were not severed.

I told Jenks that I would contact a firm of tree specialists to see if it could be raised up again. 'Oooh, you don't want to do that,' was the immediate response. The next Friday, he turned up with block and tackle and raised the tree a few feet off the ground. But he could go no further. Single-handedly, it was impossible to stop it from swinging uncontrollably on the chain, and he had to lower it. I thought then that a team from outside was inevitable, but I didn't mention it. 'Oooh . . .' was written all over Jenks's face.

The following Friday, he arrived with one of those elongated car-jacks and a boot full of large chocks of wood. Thenceforward, every week, he jacked the tree up a bit higher, inserting the wood under it. Five Fridays later, the tree was upright. He had driven a length of iron piping alongside the trunk, to which he had lashed the tree with strong rope. For further security, he had brought in cleft branches from other fallen trees to prop under the lower boughs like crutches. Not long after that epic task was completed, we had the sad news from his family that he had suffered a stroke and could work no more. He was, they said, 83 years old.

Jenks must be long gone now. As for the tree, it survives and flourishes to this day as a memorial to the old boy. Months after the accident, when the roots had settled back, it was possible to remove the props and unlash it from the iron pipe. Even more fertile than before, every autumn it produces a crop of fruits large and heavy enough to lay anyone out cold who might be unlucky enough to be passing beneath as they fall. Until I got bored with the routine I turned the hard, bitter quinces into a fine claret-coloured jelly, achieving a record yield of 62 jars one year and becoming in the process quite an expert. But that is another story, and a rather sticky one, so if you don't mind we'll leave it there.

*

A summer afternoon among friends in South Park, Oxford, 2001

One day in 2000, I received a letter from Jonny Greenwood, a member of the group Radiohead. I had heard of them but knew nothing of their music. After apologising for his 'cheek' in writing, Jonny explained that they were having a problem with one of the tracks for a forthcoming CD and, having recently heard some of my early recordings, thought I might be able to help. The band thought that something with a New Orleans flavour might fit the bill. The idea sounded to me so far out as to be interesting, so I replied, asking him to send me a tape of the song in question. When I played it, the music and surrealistic lyrics were to me utterly incomprehensible. To put it in some sort of context, I borrowed a couple of their previous albums from my daughter Georgina, who handed them over with the cautionary words, 'You won't like it, Dad.' The more I heard, the less likely it seemed that there could ever be a meeting of musical minds. Then, at some point, a phrase or nuance in what I thought was almost suicidally gloomy music struck a spark.

I met Jonny Greenwood in the BBC café at Broadcasting House, bought him a strong coffee to bolster his resistance to shock, and told him, as diplomatically as I could, that the only common ground I could conceive lay in New Orleans funeral music of the kind that, to this day, accompanies the deceased on the journey to the cemetery. Happily, he neither strode from the room nor tipped the coffee over my head, so I went further and suggested that, for an example, he should listen to Louis Armstrong's 1956 recording of the classic song, 'St James Infirmary':

I went down to St James Infirmary,
Saw my baby there.
She was lyin' on a long, white table,
So sweet, so cold, so fair.

The opening lines of 'St James Infirmary'

153

Primed with these cheering words, we all met in a studio near Regent's Park – Jonny and Colin Greenwood, lead singer Thom York, a producer from Radiohead and, from my band, clarinettist Jimmy Hastings, trombonist Pete Strange, bassist Paul Bridge and drummer Adrian Macintosh.

Despite the tentative preliminaries at Broadcasting House, it would be true to say that, when we started at two-thirty that afternoon, we had no idea what they wanted, neither did they. Lumping the two groups together, what went on that afternoon and evening can be described as a stately *pas de deux* in which we circled one another, getting slowly closer together. Seven hours, innumerable cups of tea and several incipient but happily averted nervous breakdowns later, we heard a playback; I said, 'That's it – we won't get a better one than that.' After brief discussion, Thom agreed, adding, 'Right, we'll go and have something to eat and then come back and do some more.' After seven hours trumpeting, flexing and unflexing the precious cheek muscles, I felt as if I had acquired the sagging jowls of a bloodhound. In the most magisterial voice I could muster, I said, 'Oh no we won't.'

And we didn't. After they had subsequently mixed the track, Jonny wrote to say that they were all happy. The song, Thom York's surrealistic 'Life in a Glass House', came out on their album *Amnesiac*, and I must say I'm quite proud of it. The moment when the band suddenly comes in, in funereal style, gives me a pleasant frisson every time. In his introductory letter, Jonny had said that he didn't want to use session musicians, who would just turn up, play the notes and leave. The way he put it was, 'We want it to sound as if you don't quite know what you're doing.' He certainly got that!

The Radiohead experience didn't end there. When the album came out, we performed the track 'live' on a special Radiohead edition of *Later with Jools Holland* on TV. It was the first time we saw and heard the band onstage and to me, it was a revelation. The studio was quite small, the amplification stupendous, of a kind from which, venturing too near a 'rock' tent at an open-air ball or festival, we would usually flee like startled rabbits to preserve our valuable eardrums. Yet somehow, Radiohead's music had a musicality and richness of harmony – they are schooled musicians – that made it tolerable even in the confined space.

I had seen posed studio photographs of the group on their CDs, and had found difficulty in matching what looked like a version of the Spanish Inquisition in modern dress with the friendly people with whom we had worked in the recording studio. Even so, I was ill prepared for what happened when the glowering image came to life onstage and the polite, cultured young men with whom we collaborated so comfortably transmogrified into dangerous madmen, lurching about with hair flopping and limbs flailing in characteristic rock style.

For readers who have only seen Radiohead on stage or screen, the following bit of dialogue may reassure – or perhaps destroy a cherished image. Backstage earlier in the day, I was chatting with Jonny Greenwood when his brother Colin came up:

JG: 'Have you rung Mum to say we're on tonight?'

CG: 'Not yet – if she watches, she'll only say what she always says.'

HL (unable to restrain his curiosity): 'What does she always say?

Both: 'She says, "I watched like you said, but it wasn't you."'

The following summer, we were invited by Radiohead to take part in a mammoth concert that they were staging in Oxford's South Park. They wanted us to do a half-hour set playing as we normally do in our own concerts. I think the original plan was that we would also join them in their set to perform the 'Life in a Glass House' track, but it was by then pelting with rain so the idea was aborted. As it was, I was awash with nervous adrenalin as I drove down from the motorway into Oxford in a crawling queue of excited Radiohead fans.

Then a car full of staring, pointing and, I imagined, mocking young people overtook me. When the manic-looking driver wound down his window, I braced myself against whatever ribaldry might come. Then he gave a thumbs-up sign and shouted 'Mornington Crescent!' I had underestimated the power of *I'm Sorry I Haven't A Clue* to smash down the generation barriers.

As a result, when we went onstage that afternoon, I felt almost uncannily relaxed, a feeling that not even the sight of over fifty thousand people in the field could dispel. In our set there was one moment of sheer magic. When I had put together in advance a programme of appropriately extrovert tunes, some suicidal urge prompted me to make room for our version of Duke Ellington's 'Creole Love Call'. It starts pianissimo and, by the end, falls to a whisper, prompting audiences at the back of a small room to catch up on their conversations. At South Park, those fringes, seen from the stage, were little more than blurs on the horizon.

Then, as we started Duke's familiar lilting riff, the whole field went totally quiet and almost motionless, swaying slightly to the music. Magic! It was a bonus when, in the e-mails sent to the Radiohead website by members of the audience, we were adjudged by many to be 'cool'; Kathy Stobart, my tenor-sax-playing colleague of many years and then well into her seventies, was singled out for special admiration by an audience few of whom could have reached their thirties. As for me, I was inordinately proud to see myself described as a diamond geezer.

*

Many of the nice things in my life have happened by accident. You might say that it was the accident of World War II that was responsible for most of that life itself. Before and during the war, I was steadily on course for an OK career appropriate for a young man brought up at private and public schools, with a commission in the army thrown in. I would not have been the first Old Etonian to dabble in jazz while holding down a proper job in one or other of the professions. (It was a sign of the time that only an elite catalogue of jobs was dignified by that description and art and music were certainly not among them.)

It may not have been in Adolf Hitler's mind when he set out to conquer the world, but in the event he did me a favour. By the time I came out of the army, six years had elapsed since my formal education ceased, so qualifying to follow in my father's footsteps as an Eton schoolmaster had become unlikely. I was free to become a vagabond by going to art school and playing jazz in my spare time. Thus, when the war years receded into memory (most of them, in my case, shooting straight out into oblivion at the other end), the strand that began with my childish urge to hit or blow anything from which music could be extracted became interwoven, for a while, with the inborn compulsion to draw all over any white surface that presented itself. Eventually the art withdrew on to the sidelines and the trumpet-playing became a job – no, dammit, a profession. And there I was, what Sidney Bechet used to call a 'musicianer'. Ever since, if I dwell on the careers I might have landed up in, I have been liable to wake up in the night screaming.

> The art of life is to know when to seize on accidents and make them milestones.
>
> Chairman Humph, waking from a long coma

It was through an accident that I have, hanging on my dining-room wall, a picture called *Into Oldham* by Robert Littleford.

Some years ago, before a concert in Saddleworth, my band was invited for drinks at the house of Lord Rhodes who, apart from having been, as my mother used to put it, 'very big in wool', was a patron of the arts and a sponsor of the festival at which we played. In the course of the party, I found myself close to our host, who was in conversation with another of his guests. Hearing the name 'Helen Bradley' mentioned, I moved closer to eavesdrop.

Never underestimate the power of positive eavesdropping.

Chairman Hu . . . Oh, go away. I prefer you when you're
comatose

The woman was asking Lord Rhodes if there was any artist in the area showing the natural talent of Helen Bradley, whose book, *And Miss Carter Wore Pink*, was a favourite with our children. Born near Oldham in 1900, Bradley was in her sixties when she started to paint her pictures to describe what life was like in her Edwardian childhood. Thenceforward, her illustrations and paintings, misleadingly termed 'naïve' or 'primitive' because there was no other way to describe them, became famous all over the world.

While I stood with my ears flapping like those of an African elephant, I heard Lord Rhodes mention the name of Robert Littleford in reply. Believing that a man who had framed Lowry originals stacked against the walls of his living-room must know what he was talking about, I went next morning to the Saddleworth Arts Gallery, which was showing some of Littleford's paintings.

Robert Littleford, also born near Oldham, enjoyed painting from childhood but never had any tuition. At the age of 26, he was still working on the dustcarts in Oldham when he had the urge to paint in earnest. When I went to the gallery, I knew none of this, only that Lord Rhodes had spoken of him in connection with Helen Bradley. I was therefore ready to see painting with the quality of unschooled innocence that characterises the 'naïve' genre.

What I did see, and have continued to see since with growing incredulity, was landscapes technically perfect in every way – the skies, the perspective, the capture of light, the balance of colours, composition, all those qualities that art students and members of watercolour societies strive for years to achieve – captured without tuition or study. When human figures are involved, the feeling for posture and movement is uncanny. The only 'naïve' thing about his work is the admission into his landscapes of cars, street signs, lampposts and telephone boxes, all those things that amateur landscape painters will walk miles to escape.

I left that gallery with one of his paintings. Since then, I acquired two more when I opened an exhibition for him at Salford Arts Gallery. Many will think it strange that a view of the road from Huddersfield to Oldham on a rainy day, with the water shining on a rooftop, the wheels of a car almost audibly squelching through puddles on the road, and the receding murk of Huddersfield barely discernible in the distance, should bring balm to the soul of a southerner gazing at it over his porridge each morning. But I have travelled that road so often, always in those grey and drenching conditions, that it has acquired a strange beauty, heavily laced with personal history and nostalgia.

Robert Littleford has never received more than a crumb of the recognition he deserves. But, battling with poor health, he still paints prolifically, never quite knowing how good his work is, and still with no tuition but his own intuition. That he has not been accorded another exhibition in his own area is bewildering. I am not an art critic, but I can envisage a time, in some *Antiques Roadshow* of the future, when someone will bring in a picture to be valued and will be told by an expert who has done his homework the story of Robert Littleford, the dustman from Oldham, who conjured beautiful paintings out of nowhere.

I should perhaps mention here another artist whose work hangs in my house. Luuk Add is a painter in Thailand specialising in abstract work. The picture I have is of an imaginative structure of tangled lines and shapes which, since some of the strokes are made with a dry brush and are therefore indistinct, has a three-dimensional appearance, as of twisted metal wire into which one could put one's hand. The fact that I am describing it in this way indicates that it does what an abstract should do, that is, to stimulate the mind of the viewer. It is one of my favourite acquisitions, which I have hung in my hallway where it provides, if nothing else, a talking point, since Luuk Add was three years old when he painted it, and is an elephant.

If you accuse me of stringing you along for the last paragraph, I plead guilty, but do enter a plea of mitigation. I have done it to draw attention to a worthy cause, that of elephant conservation. Luuk Add, an orphan, was rescued from the streets of Bangkok, where he survived by begging for bananas outside restaurants and night clubs (it sounds more and more Toulouse-Lautrec as we go on!). His artistic talent was discovered in the Elephant Conservation Center in Lampang.

The picture is indeed delightful, and I acquired it from my niece, Belinda Stewart-Cox, a distinguished worker for animal conservation in the field, mainly in Thailand. The discoveries that have been made about the ability of some, not all, elephants to paint consistent, intelligent and highly individual pictures are, if you look into them, rather spooky. You'll find yourself spooling back through your memory to recall if you have ever said anything derogatory about an elephant in its hearing. They have memories like . . . well, an elephant.

PS: Luuk also plays the xylophone with rhythm and flair in the Thai Elephant Orchestra established by Richard Lair in Lampang.

PPS: I guess I'd better quit while I'm ahead.

All this talk of paintings has flooded my mind with thoughts. Out with them!

Since my years at Camberwell Art School in the late forties, I have never been a regular visitor to art galleries, chiefly because until quite late in life, I did it the wrong way. Like most people, I would wander from room to room earnestly peering at everything on the walls, and nothing is more wearing to the feet than wandering. For me, it's always been striding out purposefully or nothing.

Mind you, my feet have never been much help to me since my mother took me, aged twelve, to have my hammer toes rectified. Two of the most distinguished orthopaedic surgeons in the land had a go, with operations that in those days involved plaster of Paris up to the knees, and legs horizontal for six weeks. (We'll leave till another time the occasion when I found myself, due to insuppressible wanderlust, hurtling down Windsor Hill in a self-propelled bath chair, feet foremost, arms flailing, heading straight for E V Tull's tea shop on the bend, to the horror of blue-rinsed ladies having quiet afternoon tea in the window.)

To mention the names of those surgeons in podiatrists' consulting rooms nowadays is to invoke a sharp intake of breath and much adulatory eye-rolling. Far be it from me to besmirch their posthumous reputations, which I'm sure are well deserved. But there's no other way of explaining the twin shipwrecks that are revealed when I remove my socks than to say the Mr Girdlestone and Mr Foley successively buggered up my feet in my adolescent years. And there's a word I wasn't going to use either.

It was a visit to Florence that Jill and I made back in the seventies which brought it home to me that I was doing it all wrong. The Uffizi Gallery is so vast that it was, in the short time we had on a package tour, impossible to take it all in. We decided to make a list of about four pictures in front of which we would sit, one after the other, and just stare. In the event, I don't think we got beyond the first one, finding enough balm to the soul in Botticelli's *Birth Of Venus* to last a lifetime. Anyway, we had other things to see. Balm to the soul of another kind was achieved in the afternoon when we went on one of the coach trips round Rome that the tour offered.

Sitting in front of us in the coach as we set off from the hotel was an American Shelley Winters look-alike and her daughter, a lumpish girl in her late twenties, I should guess. It wasn't long before we – and I mean the whole coach-load of us – became aware that they had suffered a mishap. That morning, the daughter had left her purse in a taxi. She herself seemed resigned to its loss, but Mom was hell-bent on tracking it down. She began to interrogate the driver, a laconic Italian with the voice and style of Victor Borge (yes, I know he's Danish, the driver just sounded like him):

'Driver, d'you know a taxi driver called Luigi?'

'Madam, there are a thousand taxi-drivers in Rome, and most of them are called Luigi.'

'But this one drove a yellow car.'

'They all drive yellow cars.'

And so it went on, until Mom began to notice statues along the route. Temporarily diverted, she wanted to take a photograph of each one as it appeared; in vain did the driver try to discourage her.

'Madam, we are on our way to see Michelangelo's masterpiece. These are all rubbish.'

'They may be rubbish to you but my daughter and I have never been here before.'

When we eventually got to confront Michelangelo's *David*, Mom and daughter had run out of film. There was a further stop so that they could replenish their supply, by which time we were running behind schedule and Victor Borge's patience was becoming frayed. In the Pantheon, Mom's anxiety regarding the lost purse returned.

'I'm gonna call all the taxi firms. Is there a phone in here?'

Victor resorted to sarcasm.

'Madam, when the Romans built this place two thousand years ago, they foolishly forgot to put in a telephone.'

Back on the coach, an argument started between mother and daughter over the location of the Sistine Chapel. Once again, Mom appealed to the driver.

'Driver, tell my daughter that chapel with drawings on the ceiling is in Florence.'

Victor's voice had become strangulated.

'No, Madam, it's in Rome and we're on our way to see it now.'

Undeflated, Mom pondered a moment.

'Does that mean we don't have to go to Florence?'

We never got to see the Coliseum. But when we got back to the hotel and disembarked, we gathered around Mom and daughter to bid a fond goodbye. There were hugs and kisses on every cheek, and watching this, I reflected on the niceness of human beings.

I began this train of thought by reflecting on the good things in my life that have happened by accident. I have a reason for repeating the oft-told story of how I stumbled upon the remarkable talent of American-born singer Stacey Kent. It has been one of the pleasures of my job as presenter of *The Best of Jazz* on BBC Radio 2 to find that, through the simple process of playing things I like almost every Monday night for nigh on forty years, I have sometimes given a boost or maybe a kick-start to the career of a musician or singer who could benefit by it.

It was in the middle nineties that a New Yorker living in London called Stacey Kent, of whom I had never heard, sent me a demo-tape, which I gathered up among some other things to enliven a long journey to Oswestry in Shropshire where the band had a gig. It happened to be the first tape that I put in my car's cassette player when I set off up the motorway. I had no great expectations – just another singer with a repertoire of standards was my thought. I was pleasantly surprised and played it through several times on the way to Oswestry and back. (I'm beginning to sound like Saul of Tarsus – not a far-fetched notion as, for me too, a revelation was involved.) By the time I got back home I had become convinced that Stacey Kent was not only a good singer, but a great one, and I said as much on the radio the following Monday. I would have continued to say it to this day even if nobody had concurred. Happily, there are now millions of people round the world who have made the same discovery.

It was some weeks after that event that we actually met. It took much less time for Stacey, and her tenor-playing husband Jim Tomlinson (also an awesome talent), to start making appearances with my band, leading to a long-running stage-show called *Between Friends*. I would be leaving out a significant contribution to the balm available to my soul if I didn't say that the chance selection of Stacey's tape on that journey to Oswestry and its aftermath has led to an enduring friendship, across the generations and across the ocean, that I can only describe as miraculous.

It's now the moment to go back to Ludovic Kennedy and bring two threads of narrative together.

In 2001, the year of my eightieth birthday, we had a concert at the Queen's Hall in Edinburgh as a celebration. The organiser Mike Hart and the festival committee had the nice idea of inviting Ludovic to the party as guest of honour, knowing that he had been the drummer in my first band at Eton. Of course, his wife, the former ballerina Moira Shearer, was also included in the invitation. When I arrived in Edinburgh the day before the concert, they told me that she was reluctant to come, since it was 'Ludovic's day'.

However, the following morning, a message arrived that they would both be there. In the course of our voluminous e-mail correspondence, Stacey Kent had told me that *The Red Shoes*, the film in which Moira Shearer shone in the forties, was one of her favourites. She was on a train travelling up with the rest of the band in an open carriage when I got the news, so I called her on her mobile. I said, 'You told me once that *The Red Shoes* was a favourite movie of yours. Well tonight, you're going to meet Moira Shearer.'

From the crowded carriage, her response came.

'OH . . . MY . . . GARD!'

That evening, we were backstage preparing for the concert when the Kennedys arrived. Having seen Ludovic not long before and heard of the cruel illnesses from which Moira suffered, I was concerned that her appearance might be distressing to those of us who remembered her in her *Red Shoes* days. It was a joy, therefore, when they came into the green room for the party afterwards, to see her radiant and, though walking with a stick, still with recognisable poise and beauty.

A little while later, I sat with Ludo reminiscing while cameras flashed and popped around us, and I glanced past him to see how Moira was faring. Stacey Kent had of course dashed over to meet her. I learned later that, on entering the room, Moira had gone over to Tony Coe, one of my musical guests on the show, to congratulate him on his saxophone playing, ending with, 'Can I give you a kiss?' If he had not already been a devoted fan, he would have become one then. With Stacey, Tony and several other admirers standing or sitting on the floor around her, the lady who had felt she would be an encumbrance was holding court. It was a beautiful, beautiful sight.

*

A little while ago we were talking about longevity and the recurring question 'How do you keep going?' When it's put to me, it's tempting, because there is no sensible answer, to be flip. A fan from the past whom I met recently claimed that when he asked that question some years ago, I replied, 'By not stopping.' I'm sure he's thinking of someone else. Nowadays, when asked the secret, I say 'Breathing,' which sounds hardly less facetious. But it's as near to the truth as I can get.

At one stage in my life, in the mid-fifties, I was well on the way to being a workaholic. My band had after eight years or so metamorphosed from part-time status to fully professional, meaning that the musicians no longer had other commitments to maintain. All except me, that is. I was no longer working as a cartoonist on the *Daily Mail,* but still producing the words (or balloon-fillers) for the strip-cartoon 'Flook', the brain child of my former musical colleague Wally 'Trog' Fawkes. On tour, I would find myself writing the words for Flook in the morning, travelling in a band coach all afternoon, doing two shows nightly between six and ten-thirty and then, as often as not, staying up most of the night carousing with members of the local jazz band. I found the answer to this lethal schedule in a book on 'Painless Childbirth' by Dr Grantley Dick-Reid who was then to gynaecology what Dr Spock was to child-raising. The book came into our house in 1955 when Jill was expecting Stephen, our first-born.

A memory intrudes:

In the trendy post-war years, the notion was introduced that it was a good thing for husbands to be present at the birth of a child. I was therefore at the University College Hospital in London when Stephen arrived. The uninvited memory is of the gynaecologist shouting, when Jill took a premature breather in the final stages, 'Come on, come on, we want more than the head!'

Idly thumbing through the Dick-Reid book one day, as part of the process of doing my bit, I came across the chapter on relaxation. The exercises involved, not dissimilar to those in yoga, seemed appropriate to my situation (though no baby was involved, you understand). It's not enough to say that, having mastered them, I have carried them out every single morning since. I have added refinements of my own (though I should warn that some readers may think 'refinement' a not altogether appropriate word) which, at the risk of sounding grandiloquent, I will call the 'Humph Method'.

Stand back, Doctors Spock and Dick-Reid, here I come!

FOREWORD. The following exercises are designed with a threefold purpose:

1. To achieve total, restorative relaxation for both body and mind.
2. To banish from the mind all debilitating anxieties and negative thoughts.
3. To offer an escape route when an unwanted caller arrives with the words, 'Yoo Hoo, it's me!' just as you are settling down with a good book. As soon as you hear the front door opening, throw yourself from your armchair on to the floor, face upwards, and start right here. Whoever it is will leave in a hurry, shouting apologies and be restrained from calling the police by the certainty that they will themselves be regarded as dangerously insane.

PHASE ONE. This can best be achieved in a prone position. I have always preferred a comfortable bed – a thin mat on the floor, as depicted in most yoga manuals, is unnecessarily Spartan and indeed out of the question when, through the passage of time, Nature's upholstery has worn thin. OK, so it's a bed. Lie on it spreadeagled, arms and legs spread. Systematically relax every muscle in the body. As the brain has little to do at this stage (it's best to keep it out of it as much as possible) let the imagination provide some figurative assistance towards a feeling that you are falling through space. Having been taken by my father to see the original *King Kong* movie in 1933 (he firmly believed that being scared witless was good for our education) I choose to visualise myself as the great gorilla in the final reel, having been shot down by the US Air Force, falling, falling, from the top of the Empire State Building in extreme slow motion, so that I could be up, showered, dressed, breakfasted and about my daily business by the time I would otherwise have splatted on to the New York sidewalk.

PHASE TWO. Once you have reached this stage approaching suspended animation, start deep breathing – and I don't mean deep sniffing. A sudden hissing intake of breath through the nostrils is useless and can damage the sinuses. Contrary to the instructions I received as a boy at Sunningdale School from Sergeant Buckle, the PE instructor, the correct method is the exact opposite of 'Come on, lads, stomach in, chest out.' If in doubt, watch a dog or cat in repose – it's the abdomen, not the chest cavity that goes up and down like a bellows.

PHASE THREE. The breathing, started when the lungs are empty, should be slow and steady. With practice, it can take as long as fifteen seconds to reach the point when the lungs seem about to burst. Don't stop there. Bringing the brain into play once more, another ten seconds or so can be achieved by imagining that there are other cavities extending as far as the collar-bones into which air can be forced. At this point – and this is where diligent practice and a steady nerve is required – hold your breath. The feeling of calm and wellbeing induced, we hope, by the relaxation in Phase One will keep at bay any uneasy feeling of imminent asphyxia. (I have a friend, a trained speech therapist, to whom I demonstrated the technique during an informal get-together at her hospital. She was interested enough to try it at home. She has not been one of my successful patients. She reported when I saw her next that whenever she reached this peak moment, chest filled, breath held, she panicked, feeling that she would get stuck there, like a kitten up a tree, unable to get down. After urging perseverance, there was no other suggestion I could make other than to get someone to call the fire brigade.)

PHASE FOUR. It's now time to come down. You will find that what I call the turn-arounds, the transitions from breathing in and breathing out and vice versa, are the hardest part of the exercise. You must try not to hold your breath so long that your eyes begin to swivel uncontrollably in their sockets and you release the pent-up air in a great rush. Think what happens when you suddenly let the air out of a balloon. Body weight and force of gravity should prevent you from actually ricocheting round the room and out of the window, but it will leave you – well, deflated and with all control gone, unable to repeat these phases several times as the exercise requires. So, start to release the pent-up air slowly and carefully, as if you were turning round on a narrow ledge high up on a building (there's the old imagery back in play). Remember, slowly and carefully. Don't fall off or you will be projected violently into *King Kong* mode, and who knows how you'll find your way back into . . .

PHASE FIVE. Having to all intents and purposes (that's tautology, isn't it? Oops, keep your mind on the job) emptied you lungs, you will be faced with another awkward turn-around. Again, slowly does it. Once you get more air in the lungs the worst is over. Go back to Phase One and repeat the whole process over again (now that *is* tautology). You don't have to hold your breath more than two or three times. Just keep the deep breathing going till you, till you . . . Eh? What time is it? Eleven-thirty? I'm sorry, I must have dropped off!'

EPILOGUE. If anxiety is your problem, I have two additions to the exercise, which I believe are exclusive to the Humph Method. The deep-breathing routine, if performed properly, will have brought about the feeling of relaxation and wellbeing. To lock the door, so to speak, against any return of bad vibes, pick a moment when you feel confidently at ease with the world, then slowly raise your arm and direct a V sign at the ceiling, uttering at the same time the dismissive expletive, 'Bollocks!' Overcome those scruples and go for it. I've tried the more refined alternative 'Fiddlesticks!' and it just doesn't work.

And the last thing. The good feeling you have attained may need a top-up from time to time through the day. If you go into the bathroom for any reason and catch a glimpse in the mirror of that old expression – the furrowed brow, the turned-down mouth, the grumpily sagging jowls, here's what you do. Go up to the mirror, look straight at your reflection as if it's another person – an *alter ego*, if you like – and give it a knowing, conspiratorial smile, with perhaps a wink for good measure, as if to say 'Nobody else has got a clue, but we know, don't we!' You think I'm joking? Well, try it – it'll take ten years off you in seconds.

Good heavens, is that the time? I started this book with a question posed by my hero, Robert Benchley. Let me end with another:

> What is the disease which manifests itself in an inability to leave a party until it's all over and the lights are being put out? . . . I can't bring myself to say, 'Well, I guess I'll be toddling along.' Sometimes even my host asks me if I mind if he toddles along to bed . . . It's that initial plunge that I can't seem to negotiate. It isn't that I can't toddle along. It's that I can't guess I'll toddle.

Well, I know the feeling. But I guess I'll toddle along now. It's been fun . . .

THE END

Index

171

Cryer, Barry 109, 110,
111–12

D

Daily Mail 2, 3, 66, 75–6,
83–4, 101, 166
Dawson, Les 78–9, 81–2
de Franco, Buddy 32, 33
Dee, Jack 95
Dexter Jnr, Dave 124, 125
Dorsey, Tommy 32, 33
Downbeat 124, 125, 131

E

Eden, Anthony 10
Edinburgh
Festival 2001 133, 164
International Jazz Festival
67
Zoo 67
Ego (Agate) 147
Ellington, Duke 36–7, 75, 86,
122, 123–4, 125, 156
Eton College 12–13, 14–19,
21–2, 25–7, 56–7, 58,
71, 102–3, 118, 132,
133, 136, 137, 157,
164

Evans, Monty 19

F

Fawkes, Wally 'Trog' 2,
166
Felix, Lenny 97–8
Fields, Gracie 79
First International Jazz
Festival, Nice 1948 84
Fisher, Charles 140–1
Fitzgerald, Ella 15
'Flook' 2, 166
Foster, Stephen 107
Fox, Geoffrey Dacre 105–6,
118
Frederick Duke of Cambridge,
Adolphus 64–5
*Freedom Principle: Jazz After
1958, The* (Liweiler)
127
Frost, David 22
Fry, Stephen 144
Fulford, Roger (historian) 57,
58, 59, 64–5
Fulford, Sibell (aunt) 47, 57,
72, 73
Fury, Billy 136

M